Edwin Courtenay

The Ascended Masters' Book
of
Ritual and Prayer

by the Lords and Ladies
of Shambhala

THE PRINCE OF THE STARS

The Prince of the Stars
is in the world but not of it.
He is the visionary and builder of a better future.
Therefore he is bringing books telling of love,
healing and a higher consciousness.

Cover Design: Uwe Hiltmann, Niedernhausen, Germany; based on an
illustration by Hans-Georg Leiendecker, Germany
www.leiendecker.com
Symbols by Graham and Edwin Courtenay
Editing and proofreading: Carole Humber

ISBN 978-3-929345-08-7

Verlag Hans-Juergen Maurer
info@verlaghjmaurer.de

———————————

*Nothing in this book
is really true.
But at the same time
everything is true,
if it is only true for you.*

———————————

Dedication

This book is dedicated to my family: My mother JOYCE COURTENAY whom I love most in life, my father RONALD COURTENAY whose love has blanketed me forever, my sister JANE COURTENAY MOORE and brother GRAHAM COURTENAY who made my childhood the unforgettable joy it was. A special mention goes to my niece AMY COURTENAY MOORE who is following in her uncle's footsteps and nephews LIAM and DENNIS, little monsters both. And lastly but by no means least to my new Godchild CHARLIE DOROTHY ELEY, a real little sweetie.
I love you all, may the Goddess bless.

With thanks to

POLLY WILLMINGTON who was present at practically every channelling contained within and was midwife to them all.
My loving friends PAUL HARRISON, MICHAEL and CAROLINE ELEY (special thanks to Michael for setting me on the channelling path), ANDREW LIDSTER, DAVID MATTHEWS, BEVERLEY HARDEN, VERONICA BRAITHWAITE and DOREEN BURGESS.
A special thank you goes to CAROLE HUMBER, my friend and aid who played a considerable role in the birth of this book by keeping my spirits up when they were low, making sure my head was screwed on correctly and checking the transcription, invaluable!!
Special thanks also go to my brother GRAHAM COURTENAY whose considerable channelling talents and artistic abilities led to the symbols for the Ascended Masters.
Namaste all.

TABLE OF CONTENTS

INTRODUCTION

by
Saint Germain

H ere is a book of magic, a book of wonder, a book of miracles. And the magic, wonder and miracle is that there is no power in these pages, no magic in these rhymes and incantations, no miracle contained in the symbols herein; but the magic and the wonder and the miracle are contained inside yourself.

From the first moment when you saw this book and touched it, something began to change inside you. From the first moment that you opened the cover, looked through the index and thumbed through the pages, something began to shift and transform within you. Your consciousness began to expand and your thoughts reached out to us here in the realms of "Shambhala," in the ascended realms where we, the Masters, exist as a composite form, our thoughts, feelings, and souls joined as one.

We are those who have gone before, who have walked upon the earth, as you walk upon it now, and through our experiences of reality have learned how to transcend the limitations of time, space and form, liberating ourselves from the need to reincarnate in order to grow and rising to this point, this other dimensional space, to Shambhala where we reach with our thoughts, power and passion down to the earth, to aid those whom we have left behind: mankind, you, to provide you with guidance, instruction, assistance and love, to be your guardians and your companions, as you walk the path of light to the glorious future which awaits you.

Although we are combined as one light, one love, one soul, we carry with us all the memories and thoughts of those whom we have been; all the characters and personalities whom we have lived through. And it is through these windows, these facets, that we shine our light, in order that we may communicate our truth to you, in ways that you can best receive it.

Therefore, it is through the window known as Jesus that we wish to speak to you of love, through the window known as Mary that we wish to speak to you of the power of The Mother, through the window known as Mary Magdalene—Lady Nada that we speak to you of joy, through the window of Saint Germain—this window—that we would like to speak to you of ritual, ceremony and magic. We are one, the same, and yet individual and separate. This is the nature of our reality here in the realms of Shambhala, where all truth is God's truth, where there is no wrong but there is only right, and contradiction is a natural path of everyday reality.

From the moment that you touched this book, your thoughts reached out to us here and we heard them as surely as we hear them now. And we reach down showering our light upon you, feeding you with our love, nurturing you with our souls, guarding you so that you may read on and use the rituals and ceremonies which we have provided in order that you may know us better and work with us more fully, as we were meant to work with each other, as brothers and sisters who walk the same path of enlightenment and ultimate spiritual discovery. But also, so that you may discover more about yourself and your own inert power, and so that you may recognise that you are God, that the Divine exists inside you as the spark which gave you life at the beginning of creation and that through this resonance you and God are one; that you are extensions of the divine consciousness, given shape and form on Earth.

The rituals and ceremonies have been created and designed in order for you to become more aware of your own divine presence, your own godly power, in order that you may utilise it to bring transformation and change into your life, to your consciousness or to the consciousness of others, in order that you may bring your world into the light, whether it is the world which exists around you personally or the world as a whole, as a universe.

The rituals and ceremonies are simple and easy. They are not complicated. Complexity does not align us to the forces of the Divine but separates us from it. The Divine itself is simple and therefore all those bridges which are to be built, which will connect us to it, inside ourselves or outside of ourselves, must be simple too.

The rituals are designed to ease you back into the practice of using ceremony and ritual, in order for you to gain access to your own inner power and in order to align yourself with our power too, so that we may guide and assist you in the discovery of the world and yourselves.

At first when you use these rituals and ceremonies, you may find some resistance which nags inside your heart or mind but this will fade in time. This is caused by unremembered memories of times when you used rituals or ceremonies in a previous incarnation and were persecuted, tortured and possibly even killed by those ignorant persons who considered rituals and ceremonies to be dark sorcery and magic. In truth, every culture and structured religion has used rituals and ceremonies since the beginning of time in order to worship the Divine and gain access to those hidden powers which exist within the world around us.

The rituals and ceremonies carry no power themselves. You are the source of energy and strength. A ritual is simply a lens, a focus, which allows your mind, your soul and the passion of your heart to be joined together in one fine point of energy, in order to make the changes in your reality possible, in order to make this change in your consciousness possible, in order for the miracle to begin.

At the beginning of many of the rituals, the Masters call for you to create for yourself a sacred space. A sacred space is formed by preparing a room in which you will not be disturbed by others, lighting candles, burning incense, playing soft and beautiful music and, with the power of the mind, placing yourself within a circle of light which you have drawn around yourself three times, clockwise.

The visualisation can be performed by opening up the chakra which hovers over the top of the head and is known as the crown centre, and allowing white light energy from the surrounding space around you to enter into it, channelling it through the body, and carrying it down through the right arm and hand by extending the first two fingers of the hand, enabling it to emerge as a beam of light or flame of light with which you can draw the circle on the floor.

The essence of manifestation is imagination and, therefore, if you do not physically see or sense anything, as long as you will it and imagine it to be, it will be so, even if you have no physical perception of its existence at all.

Visualise yourself in a circle of light or fire which ensures you protection and safety. It contains the energy formed inside it, accentuating and magnifying it. This is more than enough to begin this process of manifesting the invisible realms of spiritual reality.

It is important that this place is comfortable, the incense which you burn is pleasing, the candle light is sufficient, and there is a chair or cushion inside the circle itself on which you can sit and rest in order to meditate and perform the ritual. It is important that you have gathered together those objects which the rituals require. Although it will not matter if you leave the circle if you have forgotten something, it is better to perform the ritual in one smooth motion.

If you feel more secure or empowered in a circle which you can see, then draw the circle upon the floor with salt or mark it with stones, flowers or candles. It is important that you feel that the sacred space is real and that you do anything and everything that you can to ensure that this is most definitely the case. A sacred space can also be used without the rituals in order to meditate in, sleep, or to heal yourself or another person, or just to say prayers.

This book is a mirror and the power which you will find inside it, the magic, the miracle and the wonder, emanate and originate only from yourself. This book will guide you into ways of discovering this power. You must surrender yourself to your higher will and your heart and know that those things which it speaks of come from a source of love. Do not be afraid. There is nothing here, within these pages, which can harm you, it can only empower, strengthen, heal and awaken you.

Go forward then. Delve into this book with courage and love in your heart and peace in your mind and as you read through its pages and begin to perform the first ritual, know that we are with you. Know that our eyes watch your movements, that our thoughts guide your hands, that our hearts and souls shield and protect you. Feel our loving embrace, know our loving presence, know that we are near and close at hand. Know that we, your Brothers and Sisters of Light, are with you always and that you are never alone.

LADY NIGHTINGALE

The Ritual
of Awakening

F or the majority of us, our spiritual self is the part of us that sleeps. It is the part of us which remembers how the world once was. It is the part of us which knows the face of God and which understands that reality was created in order for us to comprehend joy and love. It is the part of us that acknowledges that all sorrow and all pain which we may encounter along the path of life are illusions or valuable teachers which lead us towards enlightenment and self-mastery.

In mankind there is a desire to understand what the source of life truly is. Mankind created complexity, philosophy and conjecture in order to try to begin to piece together the complex pattern of the Divine, thinking that by knowing what the Divine was, they themselves would truly and clearly understand their purpose for being and acknowledge and see their ultimate goal and realisation.

The truth is that the divine source of all life is not complex but simple and everything that it created is created in its own image of simplicity and therefore mankind, through its invention of complexity and by applying its complex theories to God, have themselves distanced the whole of mankind from answering the question that they pose.

If mankind is to ever truly see the face of God again and understand why we are here and what the divine source is, then we must begin with ourselves, for it is only within the self that the true answers lie. In the meantime, the spiritual side of mankind's nature sleeps on.

Although God is infinite, although energy too has no end, although the love of the Divine is like a bottomless well which is never exhausted through drawing, time is limited.

As we approach and pass the gateway of the millennium, mankind will be presented with the decision which will either lead it through the gateway to paradise, back to the long-since abandoned Garden of Eden and its true spiritual nature and its true spiritual inheritance, or it will enter through a dark gateway which will ultimately lead the earth to chaos and destruction.

If we are to pass into the gateway of light, as it has been prophesied and spoken of throughout many different cultures for many thousands of years, then mankind must awaken and those spiritual parts of our brothers and sisters, who sleep on, must be gently stirred and they must open their eyes to the new rays of the sun, of the approaching dawn of the Aquarian age.

We, you and I, are the harbingers of this new reality. We are the 'avant guard', the teachers, the scouts. It is our duty to aid all those who slumber still, in order that they may gently awaken to this new dawn and be guided to see the truth.

Awakening is not easy. Too many people have awoken too harshly in the past to this new reality and without building a firm foundation on which to stand, they have been dazzled by the light of the new sun and have fallen by the side of the path.

Others have been frightened. So frightened were they by what they saw, that their eyes now remain tight shut and they will never venture again into this light. Others, in the content of their dreams, thought that we who spoke to them of new promises and truths were mad and that we were the dream, whilst they considered themselves to be really awake. Awakening, therefore, is a delicate, fragile process and it must be dealt with with grace, love, gentleness and joy.

As we, the chosen few, journey upon our path of light, given the tasks which we are given by the Divine, the Masters and Angels, we will come across those whom we know, deep within our hearts, within our own still deep voices which cry inside our heads, that they are ready to awaken, that they must be shown the light, that they must be shown the way.

Your children, your wives and your husbands, your parents and your friends, all of whom may look upon you now as being mad and outcasts of society because of your beliefs and truths must, in time, be awoken too and although we can do nothing to interfere with their free will, we can do our best to gently stir them into acknowledgement of the truth.

In my ancient culture, it was believed that when one slept, the soul wandered far from the physical form into other-world realities: the dreamtime realms. If they were awoken suddenly, this piece of themselves which wandered could be broken from the cord which connected them to their physical form and might never find its way back. If this occurred, then the person on waking would have lost a fragment of their soul and would be weakened in power and intent, because of this missing piece.

In my culture, it was considered wise to awaken those who slept, through singing, to gently stir them with the voice, in order that their soul could hear those dulcet, beautiful tones and return to their physical form uninjured and unharmed by

15

sudden awakening, awakening as fully as they slept with all their power and medicine, their magic, intact. This is the case too, with those who slumber still to spiritual truth. If awoken too quickly or too suddenly, their spiritual selves may become disconnected from their body and they may never ever see the light of the new dawn.

The following ritual is a guidance to be used on those whom you feel have reached the point in their life where they are ready to be awoken to spiritual truth. It is no sparrow incantation which will open their eyes, give them their power and awaken them to the truth of who they once were, who they are now and who they soon will be. It is an invitation, a bidding, an evocation to the truth. It is like the song of the bird which guides the lost stranger to the clearing which they seek.

Prepare your ritual space and enter into it freshly bathed and clad in your ritual wear. Place upon your bare altar table a cloth of white and upon it three white candles burning brightly in the darkness. Allow these candles to form a triangle and inside that triangle place the photographs of those whom you would invite to awaken. As you place these photographs in the centre of your altar, pause for a while. Say the person's name and recall a fond memory which ties you both together. Smile and laugh and kiss the photo. Conjure up inside yourself and inside this space a strong resonance of connection which binds you both together through the threads of consciousness, which are universal ties and which connect all of mankind together through the web of reality.

Decorate the remaining spaces on the altar with those things which you find hold for yourself spiritual truth, epitomise and symbolise the awakening age of Aquarius: crystals and stones, pictures and books; those things which you yourself use in order to pursue that path of light which you follow.

When done, sit back and centre yourself with three deep breaths. Invoke my sign and look fondly and lovingly upon the faces on those photographs which you have placed upon the altar. Close your eyes, take a deep breath and begin to sing.

Sing the gentle tones which enter into your mind. Give these tones no words but allow the sounds themselves to become the symphony of your awakening call. Make your song low and quiet to begin with, slow and melodic, filled with the beauty and wonder of your soul.

It matters not if the tune which you hum or sing is one which you know. It matters only that you place into each note which enters into the air all the love which you can muster in your heart, all the desire to awaken these slumbering babes.

With your eyes closed, see them asleep in their beds, oblivious and unknowing of the spiritual truths and see that with each song sung, with each note uttered into the air, that they are beginning to stir, they are beginning to awaken, they are beginning to see the truth.

If you will, see lines of energy which emanate from your heart, which join you to them like threads of light and see each note vibrating along these threads of power, entering into their own minds with each round. With each verse, with each chorus, invite them to awaken. Invite them to open their eyes. Invite them to see the truth. Invite them to embrace the spiritual world.

When your song is sung, take the photographs and place them upon a clear quartz crystal, for a period of one cycle of the moon. Pay no more attention or mind to the work which you have done but allow the three candles to burn down in order that their light and wax may be spent in strengthening the invitation which you have given out to the ethers. Should those whom you have sung to choose to accept your bidding call and awaken to the spiritual truth, then welcome them with open arms into the new reality which they have so boldly and so bravely entered into.

Throw a small party for them to celebrate and be to them as your guardian angel is to you; watching over their first faltering steps upon the path, guiding them and guarding them, giving them gentle encouragement and just as much food as they need. Nurture them as you would nurture a wounded bird which you will one day set free to fly, out into the pale blue sky to embrace the light of the new sun.

This ritual and this task can be performed alone or in groups, finding a common song, which you can all sing together, to those who slumber within the circle which your bodies form. As the cockerel wakes the sun in the morning and celebrates the rise of each new day, so too must we reach out with our light and awaken those who have slept for far too long and whom we know now begin to stir gently in accordance with the grace of God. We must stir them from their sleep and awaken them to the gentle truth. As each soul awakens and sees the light of what can be, the world will become a brighter and a better place.

Therefore, when we face the gateway which leads to paradise, or the dark gateway which leads to destruction, if the majority of us then see the light of this new day, then the world will be saved and mankind will know God's own face again.

SERAPIS BEY

The Ritual of Connecting with the Angels

A s the world moves forward, mankind and angel-kind will become more and more in contact and communion with each other. The world is destined to become more aligned with the power of heaven and the consciousness of God. As angelic-kind are the messengers of God, the bringers of God's word to earth and God's consciousness, they will enable mankind to make the transition which will allow it to commune with the power of the divine Source itself directly.

The awareness and acknowledgement of angels has already begun to integrate itself more fully with the consciousness of mankind through images, stories, books, music, objects and experiences. As the earth continues in its evolution, this will become more and more apparent.

Angels have much to give mankind: understanding, teaching, truth, love, power and healing. They have the ability to make reality easy and effortless; to reintroduce to mankind the concept of non-limitation; to gently ease it back into the stream of the flow of God's consciousness; to make it aware of the greater truth which transcends that which it presently knows and understands.

In their collective mind, angels carry understanding and remembrance of what the earth once was and inside each and every one of their hearts, ideas of the beauty of mankind and its divinity. It is this remembrance which they will bring back to the consciousness of mankind in order to reintroduce them to this energy; in order to bring the earth back to a point of its past, back to a point of paradise and wonder.

Communion with angels is far easier than one would at first imagine. There is no necessity for elaborate ritual, the construction of intricate magical circles, the invocation of angels in Hebrew or Latin, astrological convergences, ritualistic ceremony and magic. Angels are around us all the time: our guardian angels, the angels who guide us in specific aspects of our work, the archangels and their attendants and the leagues of angels that transcend them. Some of their consciousness is permanently focused upon mankind's evolution and development in order to assist humans with their own growth and their own spiritual progression.

Communion with angels is a matter of intention, emotion and thought. It is a reaching out with the heart and the mind simultaneously, in order to open and expand and become aware of the fine presence of these glorious beings.

It is not an effort of our concentration but an effort of relaxation and surrender, allowing their power and their presence to enter smoothly into your life, to see them in everything, in every word, in every emotion; to acknowledge their presence as images which you will see: as statues, as pictures, as paintings, as words which you will hear whispered in the deep recesses of your heart and mind, as feelings of great joy, bliss and love.

At times however, when we are sad, sorrowful or unhappy, or when our energy, our light or our vibration is low, dark and blurred, we are unable to make this high and refined connec-

Yoke's
FRESH MARKET

STORE 18   509-928-9122
WIN A $250 GIFT CARD
FOR SURVEY   YOKESFOODS.COM/SURVEY
OR CALL 888-868-8406 TO COMMENT
Hi, my name is LINDA P 16

LEMONS LARGE		.99 FW
LITEHOUSE DRESSING		4.69 F
RANCH DRSSNG		3.99 F
SKLS CHIX TH		4.99 F
SALE SAVINGS	1.50	
BOBS FLAX MEAL GOLDN		4.69 F
SUBTOTAL	5	19.35
TOTAL		19.35
DUE		19.35
CASH		20.00
CHANGE DUE		.65
YOU SAVED ->		1.50

YOKES PHARMACY
FLU SHOTS AVAILABLE, INQUIRE @ OUR PHARMACY!
LIKE US ON FACEBOOK

02/26/2019   04 16   3:22 PM

04-454436

tion and communion; it is difficult to reach out and take the hands of these unseen helpers who can provide us with so much of what we look for and seek.

The ritual which is detailed below will provide you with a simple way of communing with angelic beings: of opening a space within your heart, in order for these glorious entities to enter into you and to fill you with their celestial wisdom and radiance.

There are a few things which you will need to do in preparation to begin with. You will need to gather together some feathers, white if possible, a mirror, circular or square, which can be laid flat upon the floor or a table top, a white or silver candle and some incense, frankincense or myrrh.

To begin with, it is important to bathe in water which has had some of the frankincense oil added to it. Relax in the bath and allow its high and uplifting energy to soothe, cleanse and banish any negativity which exists in the physical, mental, emotional or spiritual bodies. As you bathe and relax in the water, inhale this aroma deeply and allow it to enter into your body as well as surrounding your physical form. Wear clothes or robes of white. Burn the frankincense incense in the room in which you would perform your ritual and create your ritual space or circle using petals or feathers, if you have collected enough in order to create the circle in which you would work.

Place the mirror on the table top or the floor and spread around the outer edge of the mirror, so that they are reflected in the mirror's surface, the feathers which you have gathered together. Place the candle so that its light can also be seen reflected in the mirror when you gaze down deeply into it.

Before you light the candle, sit back and rest. Take a few moments to centre yourself and be still, making sure that you will not be disturbed for the duration of the ritual. Breathe deeply, relax, still your heart and your mind and release any thoughts of anguish or pain, and centre yourself.

Light the candle, invoke my sign and lean over the mirror so that you stare into it. Look at your face lit by the light of the candle and surrounded by the frame of feathers which, reflected in the mirror's surface, seem to be doubled. These feathers are the wings of angels who surround you, guarding, protecting, inspiring, lifting, healing and loving. Gaze at the feathers, gaze at the features of your face, and then gaze deeply into your eyes. As you look in the mirror, try to think only good thoughts about yourself. Admire yourself, respect yourself, honour yourself and love yourself.

If you find this difficult then think about other people or situations in your life which bring you joy, or loved friends, members of your family, lovers, husbands or wives. Try and create deep within your heart a strong feeling of joy and happiness. Then sit back from the mirror and read this prayer out loud:

"Serapis Bey, Ascended Master and Angel, guide my thoughts and my feelings skywards to heaven. Align me and bring me in communion with the power of angels. Allow them to enter into my life more fully, in order that I may acknowledge and see their presence in everything which I do; in order that I may feel them in every word which I speak; in order that I may sense them in every emotion which I feel; in order that I may experience them in my thoughts and in my life.

Draw close angels! Enter this circle of sacred space and join me in my contemplation and meditation. Draw your soft white wings around me, to protect me from the adversities of life and keep me pure, clear and safe.

Calm my worried brow with your gentle hands; lay your tender kisses upon me; soothe my mind and heart; free me from pain; enter into my life, celestial beings of light, and bring your beauty and your wonder, that I may see it and know it well."

Take a few moments to open yourself in meditation, allowing the light and the energy of the angels to enter into your life, into your consciousness. Relax and breathe in deeply and allow yourself to be filled with guidance, knowledge, understanding and love.

You can also place photographs of those people whom you feel would benefit from angelic communion and contact face down upon the mirror, so that their images can be reflected into the mirror also. If you end your ritual by doing this, then leave the mirror, feathers, candle and the photographs face down upon the mirror until the candle has burned down completely.

If you are not going to end your ritual in this way, then allow the candle to burn down anyway but gather together the feathers and keep them safe for when you need to do this exercise again.

Take one feather, however, and keep it with you throughout your day. Keep it in your wallet or your purse, in your pocket or your bag and when you have need of a special request or prayer, hold the feather in your hands, fill it with your wish or your desire and plant it in the earth as a special request and wish, which will be sent and carried to the angels.

Our love, our guidance and our wisdom, are with you always. Love is a simple and yet powerful light. Like the air, it penetrates all things, although it cannot be seen. Open yourself to the wisdom and the wonder of angels. Allow us to enter into your soul and your life and fill you with joy.

LADY MIRIAM

The Rituals of Connecting with the Seasons

I am Miriam, known once as Guinevere, High Queen of England, Priestess of the Land, Maiden, Mother and Crone of the ancient Goddess of the earth.

I bring the sweetest ritual which is the closest to the world in which you live and through which you partake of nourishment and existence itself. The ritual which I have come to give is connected to the perpetual cycle of ever-moving and ever-changing seasons of the earth which is your mother. For my ritual is the ritual of change and the ritual of the cycles and seasons of the year, the movements of the weather and the growth of the land, the transitions and changes of the faces of the Goddess herself.

Like all things which are good and true, like all things which give and do not ask for in return, like all things which love unendingly and unconditionally, the earth has become commonplace for mankind and its nature ignored. It has become taken for granted and not recognised as the miracle and wonder which it truly is.

The earth on which you find yourself is not a random and chance collection of chemicals and energies which grow in accordance with the ingredients which they require. It is not just leaves and trees, flowers and grasses, hills and mountains, streams and rivers, it is a sentient, conscious, understanding life force. It is a soul which has the shape and form of a planet, instead of that of an animal, human being or stone. It is a complex living being which combines, in balance, all the elemental qualities of its nature and existence together to form the earth, the planet, the mother, who is responsible for the creation of you all.

The earth is joined together through a collective consciousness, a consciousness which extends into all forms of living vegetation and animal life upon the planet. It is a global organism which is aware and responsive to all parts of its being, whether they experience summer, winter, spring or autumn; whether they exist separated by thousands of miles or side by side in the same forest.

The earth is the feminine force of creation, embodied as a small physical universe which we call home. It is a glorious, majestic and magical planet which endures and continues to thrive, despite the destruction which mankind has wreaked upon it, despite the intolerance of its children, despite their ignorance and their ignoring, their hate, their manipulation, their poison, their pollution, their fear.

The earth has the nature of a woman and, like a woman, embraces and loves her children who draw their nourishment from her and feed upon her. Even at the risk of her own life and survival she constantly gives until all is lost and gone. The earth moves like a woman through many cycles of being: the young fresh nature of the maiden, like the springtime; the full, powerful summer of the mother; the autumn and cold harsh winter of the ancient and wise crone.

These cycles, in an unending life, lead from one to the other: the winter transforming itself into spring, the earth giving birth in the darkness of its own womb (the sky), to its new self, young, precious and sweet. The transitions display the inner movement, the re-energising and the degeneration in the cycle of power, the need for growth and life and for death, the need for the planet to be a still and silent waste in the darkness of winter.

The perpetual, unending, ever-moving, ever-circling spiral of life echoes the spiral of the DNA structure which creates your own body, which echoes the spiral of energy in the heart and the soul, the cycle of the unending universe which moves always onwards; always in cycles, one becoming the other— repeatedly.

Although the earth is powerful and strong, ancient and mystical, knowledgeable and unfathomable to your conscious and finite minds, the earth depends on and requires mankind's nature in order to aid her with the movement of the cycles of the seasons[*].

In ancient days, in which I lived and journeyed, mankind worshipped the changes of the seasons and the cycles of the year through celebration, festivity and joy, and performed acts of magic, prayer, ritual and wishes. We aided the earth in its constant, ever-moving transformation and acknowledged the reflection of those transformative cycles inside ourselves. We witnessed the joys of spring and welcomed the sun back to the

---

* Mankind and the earth, being connected not only microcosmically and macrocosmically, are also connected through the likeness of their source making them co-dependent on each other for such things as seasonal changes and personal and planetary evolution. The above mentioned requirement refers, for example, to mankind's tendency to move from one commercial season to another, from summer sales to Christmas bargains, to Easter. This tendency has a direcet effect on reality via their powerful composite consciousness.

earth. We performed the rites in order to bring about the fulfilment of our own heart's desire and the growth of the seeds in the deep brown soil.

This was the act of summer, which displays and represents the fullness of our life, the completion of those things which we have worked hard for, the growth of the crops, the fruits of the labours of the early part of the year, the power and abundance.

Then came the darkness which moves into the summer skies in autumn. The darkness and the act of winter; the darkness and the deep sleep of the earth as the power retreats deep into the very ground itself and the earth begins to wrap itself in snow, regenerating its energy, in order that it can regenerate its miraculous soil.

We ourselves need to retreat into the light which we carry inside our hearts and, there, to look back upon the world which has slipped away from us, upon the year which has passed; to give away those thoughts which no longer require space in our heads and our hearts; to acknowledge the need to release that which once was new and is now old, in order for the life force of the planet to conserve itself deep within the roots of its own nature, in order that it may be reborn within its own mystery and power; the need to release those things which are no longer appropriate inside ourselves; to let go of hurt and pain and those whom we have loved, whom we have lost, and those who have lost us. We need to look into the darkness to find the light and the positive experiences amongst the sorrow and pain, to regenerate our own energy and begin to weave our own cocoon so that we may fly again with new wings as the sun returns in spring.

Those were the celebrations of the seasons and cycles which we performed in ancient times and which have long since been converted into Christian holidays, the true meaning forgotten and lost. This information has been given thousands of times before in books, teachings and rituals where people joined together to celebrate the flowing of the cycles and the seasons.

But in recent years, mankind has more and more forgotten the truth and abandoned the old ways. Their thoughts have turned almost solely to the need of material things, the need for money and promotion in career and profession for example. Their thoughts have urged the earth, pushed it, forced it through the seasonal changes which were part of its own natural cycle, transforming summer into winter and excluding the existence of autumn, holding on to the darkness of winter and stretching it into the beginning of spring, and then flying into the centre of summer*. Mankind's impatience, mankind's lack of honour and respect, has destroyed the natural cycle, the magical wheel of life. The echo and reflection of the seasons also causes the destruction of the natural cycle within ourselves.

The rituals which I give you are four in nature: The Ritual of Spring, The Ritual of Summer, The Ritual of Autumn, The Ritual of Winter. They are similar in their nature but altered by the context of the season which you are in. These rituals are to be performed when you feel the energy of the accompanying and appropriate month entering into the right time and seasonal mood.

Allow your senses to feel the old ripples, the old ways, the old paths and begin to abide by them, and begin to bring back into the world a little of what your ancestors used to heal the earth, and spin the wheel again.

---

* *It was recorded by gardeners all over England in 1996 that the summer green leaves of trees all over the country were falling to the earth as in winter, missing entirely the cycle of autumn, supporting Lady Miriam's statement completely that mankind's perception has direct effects upon the seasons.*

The Ritual of Spring

Wash and cleanse yourself with water which has added, to lie, to rest within its surface, the petals of roses. When you are cleansed, dress yourself in fresh white clothes and enter into your ritual space. Have upon your altar fresh spring flowers. Sit, meditate and rest, be at peace and calm.

Take a piece of paper and write upon it all those things which you wish to grow within yourself, all those things which you wish to make known: those of love, those of peace, those of hope, wishes and dreams, however large, small, or physical. When you have finished, read this list aloud and place into every word a powerful visualisation of the success and the fulfilment of your desire.

Place the paper back upon the altar and light a fresh white candle. Draw my symbol into it and speak these words aloud:

"I light this candle as a symbol of the returning light to the earth. I allow it to burn in order to evoke and charm again the sun to return. Spring flowers grow and blossoms bloom on every tree. I once again renew the power of life to this place and also within me, for I am a mirror and reflection of the earth on which I live, and I plant into the ethers of the earth the seeds of my desire in the hope that, as the wheel turns and spring becomes summer and all things which are placed within the earth grow and flourish, my dreams and desires will grow and flourish with them and find their place within my life."

Drink a little water or wine and eat a little bread as a celebration and honouring of this promise, this prayer, this vow. See in your mind's eye as you eat and drink, the light returning to the world, the power of life returning to the green, the warmth returning to the land.

Take the paper upon which you have written your dreams, wishes and prayers and plant it into the soft earth. Over it, place a little soil and then bury seeds of vegetables or flowers which you wish to grow. Over the top of this fresh mound, pour the remainder of the wine and leave the bread as an offering to the Goddess so that she may take this force of life and use it to transform the earth and make your wishes complete and real.

This is the rite of spring and, like spring itself, it is simple and sweet.

The Ritual of Summer

Once again, cleanse yourself in waters which have been filled with essential oils of lemon grass, strong and sweet. Dress yourself in strong bold colours, blue, red or green. Sit in your sacred space and rest a while, calm yourself and be at peace.

Light six candles. The colours should be green, red and yellow. Sit before their light. Draw my symbol into these candles and speak this prayer before you begin the ritual at hand:

> *"Summer is a time of completion, when the full ripeness of all things which have grown since spring is reached. The fruits are ready to be plucked forth from the womb of the earth, for the mother has grown full, and it is time now for her fruits to be removed from their place of growth and enjoyed as a child would enjoy them.*
>
> *Sun, shine hot and fill the minds and hearts of those children who you see beneath you with love, hope, joy and happiness. Open their minds, that they may see the inspiration of your blessing and do your will and work and allow the heat of summer to bring fruition and completion to all those whose lives it shines upon."*

Now you are given time to make something and complete it: a poem, a picture, bread which you can bake, a statue which you can form, music which you can write and play. Once finished and completed, show it to the candles and speak these words:

"Like the summer, I have completed that which I began and I acknowledge at this point that all work which has been done, and which is complete, must now be given away. For it is not the completed work in its finished state which carries the power but the doing, which has led to its making, the knowledge which I have gained, the lessons which I have learnt, the power which I have drawn to me and earned in this way.

I give this creation as an offering to the person who I love, to the person who needs this, to the person who I carry now in my heart and mind, as a substitute for this symbolic offering to you. They represent you in this world and they will receive this gift, as you receive my power and my love to uphold the powers of summer.

Powers of summer, fulfil me, complete me and guide me to the threshold, so that I may be ready to step forward into the next phase of my life. Draw those people to me that I must meet, draw me to those people that I have to give to, draw me to those places and those situations from which I must learn, to those things which I must endure and live through. Teach me, powers of summer, make me full-bellied and round, so that I may give birth to the fruits of my knowledge and my deeds, so that I may feel the power of the earth reflected in me."

Leave the candles to burn down and take the gift which you have created to the person of your choice. Give it to them and, as you sit with them, drink a little wine and eat a little bread as an offering to the Goddess.

Know that by giving in this way, you also give to the earth and the earth will protect those who have given to it. You will carry upon your head a blessing, all summer long, which will keep you safe from the effects of the sun and the trees and the forest which you may venture into.

By giving to the world, the world will give to you, and its protection is strong indeed.

The Ritual of Autumn

Bathe yourself in waters which have been tinged with the oils of bergamot and rosemary. Dress in deep dark colours: golds, oranges, reds and deep greens. Sit and allow yourself to enter into a state of calm contemplation and rest.

Light a golden or orange candle and sit before it. Place into it my symbol and say these words:

> *"Autumn is almost upon us and the leaves will now begin to lose their life and fall upon the earth, creating a golden carpet of beauty and light. The skies will turn grey, losing their blue and rain clouds will gather to wash the earth with tears. Darkness begins to gather and the warmth of the sun is lost. Winds will blow strong, causing cold and fear.*
>
> *This is the time of releasing, of letting go. It is the time where I must begin to reflect the earth and release those things which are no longer mine, which I have learnt from and sucked dry of life, those things which I cannot heal or help, those things which I have outgrown or which have outgrown me, those people, places, situations, those things which I may lay down to rest and leave."*

Now speak of those things for which you sought help and assistance and imagine that they are leaves which have fallen from your branches, blown by the powers of the wind.

See them one by one taken from you and feel your energy

retreating into the very core of your being to seek renewal and strength. As these leaves are taken from you, see the lessons which you have learnt, speaking them out loud, and when all is done, sit whilst the candle dwindles, wanes and burns to darkness.

Speak one more time as the candle begins to lose its light and say these words quietly:

"I draw around me the warmth of the mother's love and I stand alone in the darkness, brave, because of the light which I carry inside. Sleep still, Earth, in your carpet of leaves. Sleep and grow strong. Sleep and grow well."

The Ritual of Winter

Begin with a bath which consists of water and oils of orange, frankincense, cinnamon and ginger.

Dress yourself in a robe of dark violet, black or bold red. Sit before a black or a violet candle, light it and rest awhile. Breathe calmly. Make my sign and say these words:

"Winter is almost upon us, the darkest time of the year when the life force of the earth draws deep into the core and heart of the planet, almost so much so that it cannot be found or seen.

But I know that the darkness of the great mother surrounds me and all her wisdom, power and magic is available to me.

There is light in the night, it is the light of stars, and I am one of them, and this light has the power to call back the light of the day which rests in opposition to it.

At this dark time, I honour the power and the wisdom of death and all things which rest. I call upon my friends who have gone beyond to join me here in this realm of light. I call upon the power of the sun, the power of summer and spring which have also died, I call them back so that they may live again and return. In order to fulfil this desire and this wish, I give to the earth a gift."

Having prepared a paper bearing wishes and desires for the time ahead, familiarise yourself with these desires and show this to the candle and make a vow that you will take it to the earth and read it, sing it, perform it or bury it beneath the earth's soft skin. Then sit for a moment and open your mind and your heart to receive the presence and the power of those visitors who have come from the realms of beyond to share this special time with you. After contemplating, speak one last time to the candle:

"Candle, burn bright and call the sun back and, whilst I rest in darkness awaiting your brightness, I shall comfort myself with the light of the moon and the wisdom of the Goddess who sits by the fire and weaves.

Weave, Goddess, into my mind and my dreams, understanding of the year which has gone and been lost and allow me to see a vision of myself renewed in the future, that I may know which path to tread and what has to be done.

Give me wisdom and understanding of those things which I have not seen and give me the power to prepare myself for the year ahead."

Extinguish the candle and light it 8 more nights. During these nights, meditate and gaze into a glass of water or a crystal sphere, in order to see visions of the future which are yet to be. Wait and listen and you will hear the Goddess as she weaves the new year which is to come, telling you secrets which will help you on your way. Your power and the power of the earth are joined and connected as one. As soon as you remember and re-realise this, you will re-enter into your own divinity and begin, once again, to be enabled to share the earth with the power of the Divine Mother and live in harmony and peace.

There is great joy, love and wonder in living life in this way. Explore the nature of your relationship to the world in which you live. Grow, learn and live in love.

KUTHUMI

---

*The Ritual
of Connecting with the
Elemental Kingdom*

T he world is a living place. Everything you know and see
and take for granted has life: the grass which you tread
upon, the trees which you take shade under, the stones which
you kick down the street, the stream which gurgles on by, even
the air, the rain clouds, the thunder, lightening and fire, have a
spirit and life force.

There are thousands of beings who inhabit the forests and park-
lands of your home unknown to you, invisible to the eye,
inaudible to the ear. These are elemental beings, spirits of
ancient legends and fairy-tales, long since forgotten, long since
consigned to the realms of myth and legend.

In my life as Saint Francis of Assisi I learnt, through attunement
with the world in which I lived, to once again be enabled to
encounter and experience these elemental beings of light; to
share their secrets, to listen to their truths, to enjoy their company and lightness of spirit and to see the world through their eyes.

The Divine Source of all life, God, created all life forms in order
that they might live in harmony and peace with each other. It

was never meant by God that these streams of life should become divided in their perception or opinion of each other. It was always God's intention that they should work together for ever, aligning and attuning to each other, in order that they could assist each other in the growth of the world and the growth of the spirit. Mankind now has become so unattuned to the invisible world around it that it denies that world's very existence.

The elemental beings themselves, who long since fled to other alternative dimensional realities in order to escape mankind which hunted them and denounced them as demons sent from hell and who live in a reality not unlike our own, are still not as foolish as mankind as to deny the existence of those beings which they do not wish to keep company with.

The elemental beings acknowledge that mankind exists, even though mankind is no longer part of their world. We, in all our wisdom, should at least acknowledge the existence of their life-force presence, even if we do not desire to communicate and work with them.

However, the world would be a much more glorious place if we aligned ourselves with these invisible forces, if we worked with them in creating and cultivating our gardens, our farms, our fields; in working with the powers of the weather, in avoiding the destructive powers of the weather, in avoiding the destructive powers of fire, but utilising this force of heat and light for mankind's own good.

If we re-embraced this rich and expansive world of magic, innocence and wonder, mankind would once again find the magic and the innocence that exists inside their own hearts and their own minds that has long since been lost. Therefore, it is most important that mankind begins to reach outwards towards the living world again and re-embraces its truth.

37

In this present day and age, many vessels and many channels are speaking about elemental beings and there have been many good things written which carry a great deal of depth and truth about our elemental brothers and sisters. I shall only scratch upon the surface of this great knowledge now but I shall provide a ritual whereby these creatures may be befriended and reached out to, where we may begin to blend our spiritual vibration and enter into the realm of the elemental kingdoms.

To begin with, it is important to acknowledge and realise that elemental beings are easier to contact during the times of spring and summer than the times of autumn and winter. In autumn and winter, when the life forces of the world recede deep into the structure of the Earth Mother herself, the elemental beings retreat into their own native dimensional spaces far away from our physical earth. Some of them can still be seen and known but these are indeed few and far between.

During the time of spring and summer, the elemental beings return to our dimensional space and can often be seen or sensed in places of seclusion and beauty, far way from mankind's presence. Some elementals stray closer to civilisation and even live within the very houses in which humans make their homes, if these are void of animals and domestic pets. As they have the ability to see the elemental kind, they often try to chase, pursue and capture them out of curiosity and ignorance. Elemental beings also are afraid of metal, especially iron, because this substance has the capacity to ground or anchor their spiritual energy and make it difficult for them to return to the dimensional space which is their home. Therefore, any homes fenced in with iron, or houses containing iron in an unusual amount, will not be homes which the elementals or fairy-kinds will be friendly to.

They are drawn also to loving, gentle people, people who exude harmony, serenity, tranquillity and kindness, and often drink the milk or eat the food placed outside of the homes for those animals or birds which the people feed. Although the elemental beings do not take the physical substance itself to nurture themselves, they will take the energy of the food and the energy of the intention placed in and around the food by the person who has placed it there.

It is therefore possible to lure elemental beings into your home as you would a stray or wild animal, over a period of time, coaxing the elemental being into the home by laying down food.

Elemental beings, once inside a house, will often seek out a dark secluded place such as an attic or a cellar, or the chimney breast itself, or small dark corners of rooms. They prefer this form of seclusion, so that they are separated from humans, although often they will befriend and assist mankind with problems or difficulties or things which they need doing about the house for themselves.

If, however, you live in the centre of a town which radiates an unpleasant or inclement atmosphere, then the best way to connect with elemental beings is to take yourself to a secluded place of beauty: a forest, a park, a hill or a mountain, a place of magic. Make sure you will not be disturbed, sit down and perform this ritual.

Begin by setting yourself in harmony with the area. Listen to all the sounds which this place has to offer. Smell the air and try to take in huge lungfuls of the smells of the forest. Touch the earth and feel it between your fingers. Touch the bark of the trees, the leaves and the stones, become sensually aware of the place in which you now find yourself.

Now create a circle out of stones, logs or leaves in which you can sit. Make sure that you do not damage any flowers or trees around you but use only those objects which nature offers up to you. Create your circle, sit inside it, draw my symbol into the air, close your eyes and become sensitive to the forest once again, but this time take your senses deeper.

Reach out with your invisible mind and try to become sensitive to any presence which you may feel entering before your sacred space, your aura, the emanation of your soul which you sense around you in this place of beauty.

If you become aware of a presence, do not be frightened and do not exude fear, for this will send the elemental scurrying back to the spatial dimension from which it came. Instead, send thoughts of love and light and joy and greeting. Ask the elemental being its name and the nature of its form, whether it comes from the air or the water or the trees; whether it is a fairy, an elf or a gnome. The elemental may communicate with you with words, if it is used to humankind, or images projected directly into your consciousness.

In this first experiment, do not venture outside the circle of safety which you have created but stay well within it. When you feel that the elemental presence is wanting to depart, bid it farewell and ask it to return when you return to this space again.

Contact with any new form of life is an on-going process and therefore this ritual should be repeated until you have created quite a strong rapport with the elementals in general, or this specific elemental which you have communicated and become familiar with.

When this has occurred and you feel a strong psychic rapport has been achieved and a strong loving connection, then open the circle which you have created and bid the elemental to come inside. At this point, once you have shown complete trust to the elemental, the elemental may begin to teach and talk of things which they have not mentioned before, secret things:

magic, knowledge and power which they have. They may even offer to assist you in some of the work which you yourself are doing. It is always important to go by the feelings of the heart with each different elemental form of life which you meet.

As with normal individuals in life there are some elemental beings which are mischievous and unkind, just as there are human beings in our own society who also fall into these categories, and worse. If, however, you feel that the rapport, the being, the energy, is of a positive nature, then all is well.

When you want to take the communication further, when you want to journey with the elemental into their own dimensional space, when the elemental agrees to be your guide or offers this service to you, then draw my symbol with your mind in the air before you. It will call the conscious part of my energy to you in order that I may guide and oversee your dimensional travels with your elemental guide; it will also keep you safe and ensure that you will return to your body when the time is right. There need be no possible fear of any kind of misadventure.

Also, drawing my symbol prior to any form of elemental communication will ensure that you are working in accordance with a high form of energy which they know well and for which they have a great deal of trust and love.

From this starting point, all human beings are capable of an open, empathic and telepathic communication with all forms of elemental beings, working with them to greater depths, receiving teaching and understanding and even bringing them back into your own home, in order that they may observe you and that you may benefit from their company, too.

This is but the beginning on how to reach out to befriend and connect with the elemental kingdoms which exist around us and have existed around us since the beginning of time, to make that reconnection and to begin to benefit from that ancient and glowing wisdom.

If we are to return to the golden era which was our past and has been promised to be our future, then we must understand the steps which we have taken and, with conscious insight, re-take the routes which we have abandoned.

Sometimes it is necessary to go backwards in order to go forwards. Sometimes we must reach out and take the hands of those friends whom we met or abandoned along the way and carry them into the future with us.

We are no different in God's eyes to the elemental kingdoms. We are the same expressions of God's own divine light. We would be foolish to think that we were more important, more special. Therefore, as we began together, we must end together and we must unify with all those diverse fragments of God's will, the elemental kingdom being one of these.

Go forward and acknowledge that the world is a living one and that there are beings which you cannot see and are watching you and wanting very much to be your friends.

MOTHER MARY

---

*The Ritual
of Connecting with the
Divine Mother*

For centuries the presence of the Divine Mother has been removed from the consciousness of mankind. It has been hidden, secluded, camouflaged, presented in a less powerful and different way which has prevented access for many. It is only in recent times that the feminine force has re-entered back into the consciousness of mankind and back into the planet. This has been found in many different ways: through the rise of feminism; through the reawakening of feminine power and energy; through the conscious worship of the Goddess in all her different forms and energies and all her different shapes and sizes.

The Goddess energy is the feminine manifestation of the complimentary energy from the source that some call God. God itself is a source which is asexual. It is a source which combines both masculine and feminine energy to such a perfect balance that neither can be seen or registered. The polarity, however, still exists there and the Feminine Source can be called upon from time to time in order to provide mankind with those energies and experiences which it needs and only the Great Mother can provide.

The Great Mother, the Divine Mother, the Feminine Principle of God, the Source, is the Divine Nurturer. It is the energy which feeds our souls with what we require and need in order to exist and live. It is the power which comforts and nurtures. It is the power that loves and forgives all sins. It is the power which provides us with understanding, soft and gentle care, help and smooth healing.

It is the power which reconnects us with the energy of the universe and the earth. It is the power which provides us with hope, love, faith and truth. It is an empowering energy which can provide us with guidance in order that we may see the divine spark which resides within the core of our own heart, in order that we may re-enter the sacred temple of being divine ourselves.

It is a loving energy which transcends the love which is known upon the planet; an unconditional love that penetrates and pierces all boundaries, walls and obstacles. It is a beautiful, powerful, awe-inspiring and sacred thing.

When people are disconnected from the power of the Divine Mother, they begin to wane: their energy, their peace of mind, their self-awareness, the awareness of their own presence, their own strength, their own power. They become lost and frustrated, sick and despairing, lost and uncaring of themselves or anyone else in their immediate vicinity. It is a malady and an affliction which affects many, which causes them to lose themselves completely, which can be the undoing of a great deal of spiritual work.

It is difficult in our present day to find a place where reconnection with the Divine Mother can occur, even though the presence and the power of the Divine Mother exists everywhere. Her presence is felt more strongly at night, under the light of the moon, in places of nature, in sacred places, places of feminine worship, which have been used throughout years of mankind, to reconnect with this feminine force, this vital energy.

But there is no home for the Goddess' energy. There is no domicile, there is no special place which is now recognised, and places have to be sought and ventured to, and this makes the process more complicated and difficult, and less comfortable and safe.

The ritual which I would give then, is a ritual that will enable you to reconnect with the power of the Divine Mother, to align yourself with her energy and to allow her presence to re-enter your life. It is a simple ritual and yet powerful in its simplicity and it should be done gently and slowly, in a loving and calm way.

Gather together those things which remind you of the power of the Goddess, of the Divine Mother, things which are associated with the sea: shells, sand, starfish, pearls also, if you have them.

Also gather together some objects which you have taken from nature: flowers and ferns, leaves, pine cones, stones, crystals, objects which are connected to the planetary energy, to the feminine force of the world in which you live.

You may desire to create the ceremonial circle in which you will work out of rose petals, or flowers that have been strewn upon the floor. It is important to burn a strong, potent oil of rose which will fill your room with the strong, overwhelming smell.

Before you, have a candle which is either silver, pale blue, or pale green. Light the candle and perform the ceremony at night, in the light of the candle only. Have set before the candle a bowl of water, and also have candles that will float upon the water's surface.

Begin by centring and calming yourself and entering into a still frame of mind. Turn your thoughts inward and focus upon that part of yourself which is missing, which is no longer present. Sense it, and see it as a hole in the soul; an open, gaping wound; a piece of you which is no longer there; a part of the jig-saw puzzle which has been removed and is vacant. Feel this space and acknowledge the sorrow which it brings. Focus upon your alienation from the world. Feel your separateness, your isolation, your disconnectedness.

Draw my symbol into the air, take the floating candle in your hands and hold it, clasping it gently. Take a few deep breaths and read this prayer:

> *"Divine Mother Goddess, who is present in all the things in the world in which I live; in the dreams that work in me as I sleep; in the seas and oceans; in the streams; in the pools and lakes; in the trees and flowers; in the gentle air that I breathe; in the cycles of the seasons.*
>
> *Divine Mother Goddess, who transcends all these things: who is found in the universe and in the cosmos; who is the moon and the stars in the dark night sky, Divine Mother Goddess, you are all the soft emotions which exist within me: gentleness and caring; love and compassion; beauty and peace.*
>
> *I am your lost child; your lost son; your lost daughter, and I ask to be reconnected and taken back to your bosom, that I may suckle from your energy and be filled with your milk; that I may be reconnected to your power, and through your power, reconnected to my self, and mine only.*
>
> *This candle is a representation of my soul. Its light is lost and it is dry and beached upon the land. I light it now from your light and set it afloat upon the waters which represent the ocean of your consciousness and presence, that it may sail there, securely kept and rested in your invisible embrace until the light merges with your presence, with your ocean conscious-ness, until I am returned spiritually to your energy forever."*

Light the candle in the light of the single flame and place it in the bowl of water to float there until the candle burns down and is extinguished by the water itself. Gaze at the candle floating on the surface of the water and allow any images which form in the water to enter into your consciousness. Remember them, as they are given as guidance by the divine Mother Goddess in order to provide you with understanding concerning your disconnection and further things which can be done, in order to reconnect you with her strength and energy.

After you have gazed at the candle for some time, lie upon the floor and curl yourself into the foetal position. Rock gently, as you lie upon the floor and listen to the sound of the Great Mother's breath as it is breathed around you. Feel yourself returned to the Divine Mother's womb, safe in her darkness and her gentle embrace, no longer lost but found, no longer wanting but now provided with all your needs, kept safe within her gentle energy and her sweet love.

When you have rested here for some time, sit yourself back into an upright position and read this prayer before the rite has come to an end:

"Divine Mother, provide me with the awareness to see your presence in all things and never let my consciousness wander from the acknowledgement of your presence in the world in which I live.

May I never be parted from your side but always kept close, close to your strength and power which encompasses all the universe. For you have the power of creation within your heart and, aligned with this power, I am capable of creating every possibility in my reality. I am capable of never losing sight of the path which I walk upon, of the light which guides me there, as long as I remember and keep it close in my consciousness that you and I are joined as one. Then I will never truly be lost but always guided by your wisdom and your love."

Leave the candle to burn down and leave the objects surrounding the candle until the morning. Sleep so that the candle is within eyesight and pay note to the dreams and visions which you may have as you rest during the night.

In the morning, move out into nature, breathe deeply and experience the wonder of your world. Begin to see the Goddess in all the things which surround you and the Divine Mother in the gentle care of the land and the earth. It is important to feel your body, to experience your physical form, to wash and cleanse yourself and to gently move outwards into the world around you.

In order to reconnect yourself with the Divine Mother's presence at more regular points and periods, there is a small ritual which can be performed when the moon is full. This is the ritual of relaxation and healing, as well as communion and reconnection. This does not take place in the usual ceremonial space, but in a bath filled either with holy water or something which has been collected from a natural source, or the sea itself.

Take a deep red rose, a pink rose, and a white rose. Pluck the petals from the roses and place them in the water which you would bathe in. Light a single pink, green or pale blue candle and lie within the bathwater, with the light of the candle shining upon you.

As you lie within the water, imagine that you are bathing within the consciousness of the Divine Mother's presence. Allow the gentle energy given by the roses and the candle to fill you to the full with this power and this presence, with this strength and this energy.

After your bath, take note of the expansion of your senses and your perception. Go for a walk, eat and drink, dance, experience sensual pleasures. You will find that the sensitivity of your physical form has been extended and that your psychical senses have grown also, allowing you to reconnect with the energy of the world in which you live to a far greater and deeper extent.

The presence of the Divine Mother is not only a gentle one but can be empowering, inspiring and motivating. It is truly a limitless source of power, an ocean without end, into which we can submerge our soul and our consciousness, in order to receive sustenance and nurturing to an unimaginable degree.

It is a power which must not be tapped into lightly, for it is close to the magical universe and once filled and reconnected to this power, you will find that you are more magically potent, more capable of performing feats of healing or sensitivity. You are awakened and reconnected with the deep currents of the universe's nature and your thoughts will manifest and materialise far quicker than they normally do. Therefore, it is important after reconnection with the Divine Mother's energy to be cautious in the manner in which you exercise the power of your heart, your head, your physical strength, and to wear your power lightly, balanced always by the heart.

Remember that the Divine Mother is never far but to be found in all things, so use these rituals to reconnect yourself with this strength and this beauty.

JESUS

The Ritual
of Connecting with the
Divine Father

The nature of God is simple. It is an energy which is conscious, which carries intelligence, knowledge and understanding. This energy is fully aware of what it is. It knows itself extremely well. It is this ultimate self-comprehension which inspired God to create reality and limitation in order to advance and learn.

It is this self-knowledge which inspired God to create mankind through which knowledge could be received of earthly limitation and reality through experiences, which God himself could not make, so that they could be integrated and understood more fully.

God, the Source, is in truth neither male nor female. It is a composite energy, bearing a polarity which is so finely integrated that it can neither be sensed nor seen. It is neither black nor white, good nor evil, male nor female, but something which transcends all these things, although, in principle, a polarity of energy can be called upon and attuned to more fully.

When we are disconnected from the masculine aspect or

attribute of God, the Source, when we are disconnected from the Father, then we are lost. The Father is the motivational aspect of our own soul. It resonates with that part of our own spirit which guides us and inspires us and motivates us to continue to learn, to grow, to search and discover; to seek the answers to our own questions; to find the end of our journey; to continue with that journey, no matter what the adversity, the difficulty, the pain or the sorrow.

When we have lost our connection to the Father within and the Father without, then we ourselves are floundering. We have moved off the path of light, out of the stream of the Divine Mind and we are lost in the limbo of guidelessness, hopelessness, pain and confusion. It is easy to become disconnected from the Father, far easier than becoming disconnected from the Divine Mother energy.

The Divine Mother energy is all around us. It exists in nature itself. It is beneath our feet. It is in the tree that we lean upon, in the air that we breathe. The Divine Father's energy is more invisible, less tangible, more a force which is based upon faith and belief in the invisible, rather than the acknowledgement of something which can be seen and felt, touched and tasted.

It is important, therefore, when we feel lost and are floundering, when we no longer contain the spark inside our hearts necessary to provide ourselves with the motivation and power which we require to continue the battle of life, that we seek to reconnect ourselves more consciously with the power of the Divine Father, of our Father God.

It is at this time that we must re-address our focus and pull ourselves back to the path of light and into the stream of the Divine Will, in order that our life can flow again, in order that we can flow in the direction of the stream and move more fully into our own potential and our own purpose.

Therefore, the ritual which I will provide you with will enable you to reconnect with the power of our Father God. It will reconnect you to the Divine Will which exists within and without, the motivational force of the consciousness of God.

It will enable things to flow more fully in your life and thus may have the effect of providing you with healing or reducing obstacles which exist within your path, or providing you with the guidance which you seek from others, from situations, places or from within. It may also energise you if you feel that your own energy is severely depleted or lost. It may provide you with the miracle which you have been searching for, or the faith which you feel you have lost.

This ritual and ceremony should be performed when the sun is at its highest point in the day. It should be performed out in the open or in a room which allows a great deal of light to enter into your space. If at all possible, also allow fresh air to enter into the room and try to perform your ritual in a place where you can hear birds singing or trees being blown gently by the wind, or the sound of a stream nearby.

Create your sacred space and burn a light and fragrant incense, an incense which smells like flowers, an incense which brings you joy and happiness: a light gentle incense which makes you feel connected to the world.

Perform your ritual before a single white candle which has been anointed with the same incense which you are using to create the aroma in your ritual space. Sit before the candle for a few moments and relax, making sure that you have created your space correctly and making sure that you have prepared yourself so that you will not be disturbed.

Relax and be still and breathe deeply for a few moments. Listen to the sounds of the birds outside, the sounds of nature, the sounds of your home. During this time, allow yourself to fully explore those difficulties which you are experiencing: the blockages in your path; the impasses which you are journeying through; your disconnection to God; your lack of faith; your lack of ability to believe.

Relax and explore these sensations and feelings with the fullness of emotion. Do not be frightened of becoming sorrowful or depressed or tearful. Explore the dimensions of these emotions fully. Bring them to the surface of your consciousness and your understanding.

Having previously prepared a chalice full of purified water, take the chalice in both hands and hold it at the level of your heart. Take a few deep breaths and repeat this prayer aloud:

"Divine Father, I sit as always before your presence but, at this time, I am in need, for I feel that I have lost my way upon the path and can no longer feel your guiding hand. I do not know how far away I am, nor how near, but I am aware only of the feeling of your absence in my heart and in the world in which I live.

Guide me and pull me gently back beneath the light of your wings so that I may feel your breath upon my neck, your gentle hand upon my shoulders, so that I may hear the beat of your heart and feel the tenderness of your embrace, so that I may feel you within and without, and gently glide with grace once more upon the crest of your fast-flowing stream.

Guide me from the darkness, out of limbo, into your light, and provide me with the direction which I seek and need.

In my hands, I hold the chalice, the symbol of your love and light, bridge and ladder, which joins my heart to yours. As I drink from it, then may I also drink from your power and your strength, from your wisdom and your love, and may you fill me as the water fills me and connect me to your limitless source of light."

Sip the water gently from the chalice and follow with your thoughts the water as it journeys deep into your body. Take a second sip of water, and then a third, and then place the chalice back before the candle.

Relax and close your eyes and visualise a stream of light which issues from above you and which engulfs your entire form. Within the stream of light there is a ray of pale pink energy which enters through the crown centre of the body and journeys down the etheric spine, piercing all the chakras until it reaches the heart. Here the beam of light attaches itself to your heart centre and connects the spark of the Divine, which exists within the core of the chakra, to the Divine Source of God. Feel this as a strong tie which cannot be broken: powerful, invulnerable and yet gentle.

Relax in this powerful embrace, releasing all fear and tension, all concern and all worry, allowing all negativity and dark thoughts to flow from you, cleansed and eased by the passage of this light. Relax into this power and open your mind and your heart to the guidance which will be given, to those things which you would see and know.

You may sense the presence of angels or my presence, or you may sense the presence of God the Father himself. Be open to the miraculous ability of your own sensitivity, to become aware of the hand which is extended to you at this time. Feel protected and comforted.

Say these words after you have relaxed for a while, within the space of this energy:

"Mighty presence and power of the Lord Father God, I welcome you into my heart and the space of my life.
I shall try to see you, sense you and hear you in all things and, as I extend my hand to you, then also extend your hand to me.

So that we may walk hand in hand along this path of light which is my life.
So that I may know that you are always there, even when it is most difficult to see you.
Guide me and give me a sign of your presence and your power that I may know it to be the truth.
This is my will and if it flows in accordance with yours then allow it to be so. So mote it be. Amen."

If you feel you would benefit from lying down and sleeping for a while, surrounded by the presence of God, then do so. If you desire to meditate further, then do so. If you desire to ask for specific guidance and assistance with problems which are presently in your life, then do so also. If you would like to send healing to another person, then now is the time for this, too.

When you have finished, allow the candle to burn down completely. Then take the water and pour it into the earth, anchoring the presence, the power, and the wisdom of God into your physical environment and locality.

Keep your eyes and your ears open for the presence of God in your life. His presence will make itself known.

Keep your heart open to the receipt of miracles for these will often occur in order to provide you with belief and faith. Open your mind to the guidance which will be shown to you and live in faith and in trust.

This ritual is simple, like the Divine itself, and yet it is no less powerful because of its simplicity. It can be performed anywhere and at any time if the need arises, although the details which I have mentioned will enable you to perform the ritual at its optimum.

Remember that the presence of God is with us always, even when it can neither be seen nor felt. It is like the air which we breathe, invisible, unmeasurable but ever present and all-penetrating. Carry this gentle wisdom in your heart and, in times of need, allow it to reassure you of this truth.

LADY PORTIA

The Ritual of Initiation

I am Lady Portia, Lady Ascended Master of completion and initiation, joint custodian of the silver violet flame of transformation and spiritual alchemy, harbinger of peace and ending, bringer of dusk and completion of a hard day's work.

I am the guardian of all those things that wait. I am the watcher on the way who stands at the gateway to the new Aquarian age; the protectress who prevents all those who are not ready from passing through the gates of initiation which will bring them new life and understanding. I am, at times, seen as a shadow, dark and fearsome, challenging and evil. But I represent and uphold that which must be transcended before it is known that a neophyte is ready to become a priest or priestess, before a boy is ready to become a king, before a seeker is ready to become a co-creator with the power of the Divine, a champion of light.

Without challenge, no form of reward can be truly relished and savoured. Without resistance, no forward flow could be enjoyed. Without the control of the teacher's hand who presents the examination paper to see if the student has learned his lessons well there would be no sense of accomplishment.

I represent the archetypal forces which govern and restrict evolution and forward movement. I am the initiator through all steps and walks of life, whether the initiation is ritualistic and spiritual, whether it is the triumph of a physical accomplishment, running to the top of a mountain, whether it is an emotional triumph, opposing someone who has always stolen away your power, finding your own strength, going your own way, whether it is a mental success, overcoming a problem that has always stumped you and caused you concern, I represent those things which can be transcended and the ways through which transcendence can be gained.

In the lifetimes which I have led, I have often played the part of the darkness, of the temptress or the enchantress. The power which I operate with and through has been known in many cultures. In India, as Maya, the power of illusion; in the native American cultures as coyote-medicine, the trickster or the sacred clown, the Heyoca; in Tibet as the demon of all that is not real; in Christianity as the devil. But all these forces and forms of darkness and shadow, of illusion and confusion, are simply temptation, challenge, resistance, test. They are teachers which gauge the competence of your heart and mind, to see whether you are ready to progress and evolve, and reap the benefits of the grass so green which lies on the other side of the bridge.

I am the troll who tests the Billy Goats Gruff. I am the giant who guards the magic harp. I am the wicked witch who prevents Dorothy from finding her way home. I am the second path which lies before you, which tempts you to journey deep into the forest where the wolf lies.

I am not evil, but I am at times dark. These are two different things. My role, my purpose and my function, is only to see if you are ready, for if you are not and you are allowed to pass through the gateway into the other realms of your own evolution, you would be destroyed, consumed by power which you are not yet capable or ready to handle or work with. I am the divine fuse, a safety valve, which prevents you from entering into those realms which you are not prepared for. I am the lock, and if you are ready then you are the key. Initiation happens many times throughout our lives and in many different ways. Some initiations take place daily and slip past consciousness unnoticed, due to the business of society, its pace and speed.

Any form of triumph and success, enabling you to do something which you were previously unable to do, is a form of initiation. Any trauma or horror which you have passed through, however you passed through it, is a form of initiation. Any journey or adventure, any exploration into the unknown, is an aspect of initiation: beginning a new job, starting your first day of school, sitting an examination, driving the car in busy traffic, baking a cake which you have never baked before, teaching, guiding, guarding, becoming a parent, grieving someone whom you have lost, being given power and learning how to use it, building a shelf, learning to operate a computer, learning to use the hidden skills which exist inside your heart and mind, painting a picture, writing poetry, composing music, watching as one season becomes another, celebrating Christmas or Easter, having a birthday or an anniversary, remembering someone who has died.

These are all possible opportunities for initiation, points of transformation, which, once you have journeyed through, will take you to an inner space which you have never been to before and which will make you into something different, something new. Even if you fail the test, you have still experienced the elements of and possible opportunities for initiation, but have simply not gained the rewards, the benefits which lie beyond it. Nevertheless, the experience is no less valid. Everything is teaching, even pain, often even more so than joy.

So darkness is not truly bad or evil, but simply another way of experiencing life, another way of growing, another way of evolving, another way of gaining power and journeying closer to God.

Once upon a time, long ago, initiations were a common-place occurrence. They were acknowledged and utilised powerfully, at all moments throughout life: the birth of a child, the conception of that child, the joining of a couple in marriage and their first night together, the child's coming of age; its birthdays and its first day as a working member of the community, caring for the fields, greeting the sun in the morning, greeting the moon at night, calling for rain or wind, calling for good fortune or joy, turning the wheel of the year, calling upon the power of the universe to aid in daily life.

It is only now, in today's society, that initiations and rituals have become lost or minimised, their power stolen and weakened, turned into fantasies and folklore. But this does not mean that their power has been lost or faded away, but simply forgotten. It lies waiting in rest, like a hidden treasure, and all that you have to do to find that treasure, to open the casket and to benefit from the riches and the power, is to begin to acknowledge the need for initiations in your life, in order to flow more fully and prepared into all the many varied stages which your existence offers, however trivial or however great, however mundane or however spiritual, however small or however large.

Here follows the basic formula for an initiation which you can alter and change in accordance with the particular form of initiation which you are at present facing in life.

First of all, you will find a ritual which will prepare you for your initiation and, the second ritual, which will also be given, will be a "post-ritual" enabling you to complete and stabilise the transformations and changes which you have experienced within yourself.

Begin by bathing in water to which have been added three drops of patchouly oil, three drops of lavender and three drops of rosemary. Bathe in the water by candlelight and allow the rich smell of the oils to gently enter into your skin, into your mind, into your heart and into your soul. Imagine that the water is taking away from you any negative or unpleasant energies which you have gathered throughout the day.

The oils are placing your consciousness in a particular inner space, a magical and enchanted realm, a dimension of initiation, transition and change.

After you have finished bathing, dry yourself and dress yourself in a robe or clothing which is black. Journey to the outer physical space which you prefer to prepare for your ritual and begin to gather together the things which you will need, and settle yourself down. Burn a little patchouly oil or incense, play some delicate and gentle music which is emotionally evocative but soothing, and light some black or deep violet candles, nine if possible.

Have prepared a metal basin, something which you can burn something in and also a recent photograph of yourself which you no longer want or require. You may need to place this dish on a tile of wood or clay which will protect the floor from heat. If you would like, you can gather together some lavender and some amethyst stones.

Sit before your altar space which you have placed the candles upon, the bowl, the photos, the herbs and the crystals and take a few deep breaths, centring yourself, calming yourself, preparing yourself. Think about the past and the situation which has led to the change and transformation which is about to be made, the impending initiation which you are about to journey through.

Allow yourself to fully experience any emotional disturbances: joys, fears, worries or concerns. Cry if you will, laugh if you will, smile if you will. Explore these as fully and as deeply as you can, whilst holding the photo between your hands. Draw my symbol in the air and invoke me in this way:

"Lady Portia, Lady of Shambhala, Lady Ascended Master of Initiation and Completion, I call upon your power and your presence, to bear witness to this ritual, to this initiation; for I begin a journey which will take me forward to an inner space, which I have not been to before, and I shall be changed by this journey in ways which I cannot begin to comprehend.

I am frightened and I am full of expectation, and I am joyful, but I feel alone, a little lost, and I need guidance, protection and assurance on my way.

Help me and guide me forward, allow me to see inside myself the strength which I require and need to fulfil this initiation and to be triumphant in my desire."

Take a photo and burn it in the metal bowl which you have ready, allowing it to burn completely. As the photo burns, place some of the lavender over it and take the amethyst crystal in your hand. Watch the burning photo and make sure that it burns completely, until it is only ash. While watching it burning say these words:

"This photograph is a symbol of my old self. As the flames consume it let it pass away, let my old self pass and be reborn."

Then sit back and close your eyes. Try to clear your mind, allowing any mundane thoughts or images to float freely through your mind, as if they were clouds passing across the sky. Try not to be too harsh or severe with them. Now try to take note of any thoughts or feelings or images which enter into your mind and note them down, as soon as you see or feel them.

These thoughts are given to you as guidance and even if they may seem mundane or strange or inappropriate, it is still important to take a note of them and to carry them with you, as you journey through the initiatory stages of your life, in order to see if their messages have hidden meanings which you will recognise and appreciate at a later time and date.

When no further images appear, place the amethyst back on the table, sit back and rest again, taking a few more deep breaths. You have begun your journey and aided yourself in the transformation which will inevitably take place. Extinguish the candles and finish the ritual by burying the ashes of the photo in the earth to ensure and aid the transformation on the physical level and go on your way in peace.

At a later time, when you feel that you have journeyed through the initiation and you feel that you are nearing completion, take a similar bath but, this time, place beneath the black clothing which you will wear, white clothing or a white robe.

Journey back into the outer physical space which you have prepared, lighting once again the nine candles of black or violet which you have used in the first part of the ritual. Have the amethyst upon the table but, this time, no bowl and no photograph. Light the candles, draw my symbol and address me in this way:

"Lady Portia, Lady Ascended Master of Initiation and Completion, I have journeyed through the darkness and uncertainty of my initiation and I now seek completion. I now seek to reach the end of this journey, so that I may rest and use the power and experience which has been granted to me and find peace, balance and harmony.

Grant me the power and the knowledge to comprehend the lessons which I have learnt and to use the wisdom gained wisely. Give me the understanding that I may know whether I have suc-

cessfully absorbed that which I needed to learn and understand and enable me to grow and blossom in fullness, love and light."

At this point, take off the black outer robe, so that you remain sitting in the white robe and state:

"I have entered the darkness and journeyed through it into the light. I am no longer the person whom I once was, but I have changed. I have transcended that part of my nature. I have learnt my lesson and entered into a new state of being and power. I have passed through this initiation in this particular phase of my life."

At this point, it is important to decide to journey and to buy yourself something which will serve as a token of the transformation and initiation which you have passed through, something to wear or a piece of jewellery or clothing; to cut your hair, or to change its colour, or to alter your appearance in some small way; something that will serve as a physical acknowledgement of the transformation which has taken place, so that you can look at it and remember the initiation which you have just journeyed through.

Please feel free to alter the ritual in accordance with the particular initiation which you are experiencing. If you are leaving something behind, then burn a picture of it or the person, when you burn the picture of yourself. If it is a celebration of a coming of age or an anniversary, then incorporate that too, with singing or with a cake or a gift. If it is an event of grieving, then incorporate a picture of the person whom you have lost. Address them and ask them to watch over you and guide you through the initiation of their loss.

By meditating, you will find ways of adding to the ritual, in order to personalise and modify it, and which are appropriate to that particular initiation which you are journeying through.

Although the ritual is simple in its form, you will find it powerful in its effect. You will find that it will be an acknowledgement and inner confirmation of that which you are inwardly experiencing.

You can finish the ritual with a celebration or with quiet contemplation by writing your experiences down, by going for a walk, by spending the evening with friends. It is important to let the candle burn down completely in safety.

You will find that by highlighting the initiations in your life, you will be making clearer, definite chapters, highlights, points for future reference, on the map of your life's plan which will enable you to more clearly pass into the new stages of your existence.

Initiation is a powerful experience which causes deep transformations to occur on all levels of being. Initiation guided by another person is powerful, but self-initiation is more so. It is allowing and surrendering to the Divine, giving your consent for an inner transformation to occur, which will ultimately bring life and love. However sad or difficult, however painful, initiations ultimately always bring light.

Go then in peace and joy celebrating these monumental moments in your life, knowing that, from one moment to the next, you will never be the same; knowing that life is an initiation in itself, every day, every moment of that day, carrying within it the magic and the power to transform you forever, to alter you subtly and greatly and to bring you closer to the divine potential of who and what you are.

I end with a prayer, dedicated to the universe, a prayer which can be used for yourself or which can be spoken gently to another who is experiencing a point of initiation in their life; a prayer which can be passed on in a greeting card, for those who are not yet ready to begin to explore the spiritual potential which exists inside themselves and would feel frightened of rituals.

The prayer carries inside it the consciousness of initiation which can help raise the awareness of all those whom it touches:

"Divine light, which carries many shapes, colours and names, look down upon me with loving eyes as I journey on my path, for I am faced with an experience which is challenging, painful and joyful.

This experience is a doorway which carries me to a place which I have never been to before, and I am frightened. Assure me of your love, wrap me in your soft wings, so that I may know that wherever this doorway leads, I shall never truly be alone but always have your light to guide and love me, to assure me that no decision is ever truly wrong and that there is always light inside all darkness which can be found. Initiate me then, Divine Source, Mother and Father of Life, anoint me and carry me forward in grace and surrender to a better time, a better place, a greater me, that I may continue to blossom and grow forever in eternal light."

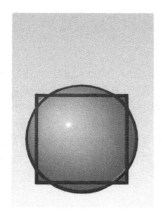

EL MORYA

The Ritual of Protection

I am El Morya, once known as Arthur, King of England, Lord of Shambhala and Ascended Master; bringer of the will of God to earth; bringer of strength, protection, harmony and peace.

Protection is a difficult issue to communicate. To many it is an unnecessary procedure that attracts darkness and creates problems rather than solving them and protecting against them. Some firmly believe that the act of protection actually attracts the darkness in various ways and that by simply remaining faithful and trusting in God, it would not. Others testify and believe that the act of creating protection also creates the evil that assails against it and that all darkness is merely an illusion. Others still claim that we should have simple and ultimate faith in our guides, in God, in the Masters and Angels that watch over us and protect us. This, in itself, is true but you are beings who still remain bound to the earth with all its laws and limitations and you must take responsibility for your own lives, and you must understand and believe that the darkness does indeed exist. It is part of the universe and part of the Divine.

To say that the darkness is merely an illusion is to say that the light itself is an illusion, and this is not so. As we have seen and discovered, the darkness is not evil but the darkness will do whatever it can to try to prevent us from reaching the evolutionary goal that is our destiny. And if that means employing those who carry evil within their hearts and minds, then so be it.

So we must take responsibility for ourselves upon the earth. Yes, we must call upon assistance, aid and protection from the Masters and Angels and all those spiritual beings that surround us. But we must do what we can to provide ourselves with the form of protection that will keep at bay not only the spiritual but also the darkness that assails on the levels of the heart and the mind, and indeed the body itself. In order to be safe and secure, we must cover all areas of existence that we may not be tampered with, controlled, manipulated, drained, attacked and weakened.

Many would say that the best way to protect yourself from the darkness is to transcend it, and this, of course, is true. Low level entities, elementals and suchlike, which assail from the lower vibrational dimensions can simply be overcome through transcendence. Transcendence is lifting the vibration through joy and happiness to a higher spiritual plane. It is a simple enough exercise and can also assist you in protecting yourself from negativity of a mental, emotional or physical level. When you find yourself in the company of someone who is emotionally or mentally disturbed or confused, who carries a great deal of negative energy on these levels of their personality, or someone who is physically sick, then you can remove yourself from the influence of these lower vibrations or conditions simply through exercising joy and happiness.

It was in the fable of Peter Pan that he managed to fly by finding a happy thought. This is the same in your reality. If you want to fly, to soar in the higher spiritual vibrational dimensional realities, then you must find your happy thought. You must find the joy that exists inside your heart and you must focus upon it. A memory of a happy time, a person whom you love, something that brings you joy and happiness, even if it is food or a place. Find your happy thought. Hold it in your mind, a light radiating out from the heart like a warm wave of energy. Allow yourself to smile or laugh and feel yourself gently lifted above and beyond the realms and this darkness.

However, the darkness does truly exist on all vibrational planes, only in different forms and disguises. So even if you raise yourself to a higher vibrational frequency, you will simply be facing a darkness which is in a sense more powerful, more extreme and you must be prepared for that. There is only a certain limit or extent to which your vibration can rise at any one given point in your evolution, and maintaining that state of joy and happiness is difficult, but there are other ways to protect yourself.

In the era in which I lived as Arthur, protection was simple. To those who lived in a physical world, protection was a good shield or suit of armour. It was a castle with strong walls or deep moats, it was good men and women, it was a fast horse, but for those who lived in that time on a spiritual and magical level, like the counsellor who was my friend and family, Merlin, who is now the Ascended Master Saint Germain, protection was also a magical and spiritual thing, a thing performed with a ritual and prayer, calling upon the power of deity and archetype.

The ritual that I am about to give you is a combination of the two. It is utilising symbology from my own era of kingship: the image of the sword. Some may say that this ritual is complex, and indeed it is, but once the ritual has been practised a certain amount of times, it will become easy to remember, it will be fluid and smooth, and you will undoubtedly feel the power of its protection.

If you have the time to prepare yourself properly for this ritual, then you should take yourself to a nice, warm bath and place in it five drops of frankincense oil. Bathe in the water and allow the rich and heady aroma of this oil to soak into the skin of the body and enter into the nostrils. Breathe deeply down into the physical form, dress in clean clothes, and enter into your ritual space.

Light before you a single candle, white, silver, gold or violet. Take a few moments to pause and breathe, to calm yourself and to become still. Make sure that you won't be disturbed so that your entire focus and concentration is upon the exercise that you are about to do. Once the exercise and ritual has been started, it is well advised that you do not stop until you have finished; by half completing the ritual you will weaken its power and may allow a negative energy force to enter into the sacred space which you are creating as a mobile dimension of protection around yourself. Because of this, it is equally important to make sure that the space in which you are working is a good, clean, sterile spiritual and physical environment. Cleaning the room that you are about to work in will help accomplish this on a physical level. Burning a little frankincense, lavender or sage in the room will also help to cleanse the environment. It will make it spiritually clear to raise the vibration sufficiently that it may help you with the visualisations that are required.

Begin by imagining before you a five-pointed star being large enough for you to sit in its centre. Imagine the tallest point before you, so that the two other points extent right and left in front of you, and two right and left behind you. You are sitting within the centre of the pentagram facing the top point. See it clearly, defined and strong in your mind.

Now begin by visualising a sword in life size and held in your hands. Visualise it formed out of a violet light and place it so that the blade points outwards on the top point of the pentagram in front of you. As you place it there, sit back and say these words:

> *"This is the sword of Azrael, Archangel of Spirit, creator of all angels of the elements. It is placed here to protect me from all things that assail on the spiritual dimensions of life, to keep me safe and protected, asleep or awake."*

Next imagine a second sword made from a rich green light, like the green of deep forests. Place this to the right of the sword of spirit, on the point of the pentagram that stands slightly to your right. Place it down, sit back and repeat these words:

> *"I call upon the power of the sword of the Archangel Uriel, Archangel of the earth, Lord and master of the secrets of the planet on which I live. I call upon your strength and wisdom to guard and protect me upon the physical planes, to keep me safe from all physical harm and accident that should occur, asleep or awake."*

Turn your body to find the third point of the pentagram behind you. Visualise the third sword forming from a light pale blue energy. Place the sword down in front of you, sit back and repeat this:

> *"I call upon the power of the Archangel Raphael, Archangel of the air. I call upon the power of his sword to protect me from all those things that assail on the mental level, thoughts that exist within my own mind or thoughts that are projected to me from others. I call upon the power of this sword to keep me in a state of healing grace, to keep me well and clear, as I wake and dream."*

Turn to face the fourth point. Visualise a sword forming in your hand, made from the rich, fiery embers of the sun. Place it before you, sit back and repeat this invocation:

"I call upon the sword of the Archangel Michael, Archangel of fire. I call upon the power of passion, the power of love and the power of spiritual alchemy. I call upon the power of the hero of God, the power of light. Protect me and keep me safe from all things that assail the spirit and the heart, keep me safe during times of transformation and protect me in the between-times when the veil is thinnest. I call upon the sword of Michael to protect me, as I wake and dream."

Turn to the final point of the pentagram and begin to visualise a sword forming, manifested from the watery greens and blues of the ocean. Place it on the point in front of you. Sit back and repeat this invocation:

"I call upon the sword of the Archangel Gabriel, Archangel of the water, Archangel of dreams, Archangel of the heart, keeper at the sacred Chalice, the Grail which contains the mystery of the great Divine itself. Gabriel, protect me as I sleep and dream, as I wander from my physical form into the astral planes at night. Keep my heart clear and pure and extract all evil that exists there, that could be used against me. Shield me from emotional harm that could exist from all others. Keep me safe, as I wake and dream."

Turn yourself so that you are facing the sword of spirit, the first sword which you have placed, and pause a moment. Feel the power and the energy around you. Now you are going to place five more swords by the sides of those which you have already planted in the earth before you. Each of these swords will, once again, have blades pointing outwards. They will be placed between the swords that are already existing upon the earth around you.

Imagine in your hands a sword beginning to form forged of pure light, as if it were made from the very heart of the sun itself. Place this sword between the sword of spirit and the sword of earth. Sit back and repeat this invocation:

"I call upon the sword of light that represents the Divine itself. Light, which is the bringer of life. Light, which is the ultimate future and destiny. Light – which is power and strength. Protect me, power of light, as I wake and dream."

Visualise, forming in your hand, a second sword. This sword is created from the most vivid and beautiful, pink light. It is to be placed between the swords of earth and air:

"I call upon the sword of pure love. I call upon the power of the heart. I call upon the unconditional energy of the Divine to guard and protect me on land or at sea, no matter who and what I am, to keep me safe in love."

Place the third sword which begins to form in your hand between the swords of air and fire. This sword is made from a silver light that glimmers and shines. Put the sword down. Sit back and repeat this invocation:

"I call upon the sword of truth which pierces all illusion and lies, the sword that protects and defends the power of realisation and enlightenment. Sword, cleanse and clear my mind that I may see the light, that I may ignore the darkness, that I may be guided to all those who love me and can teach me, that I may be guided away from all illusion and trickery, as I wake and dream."

Between the sword of fire and water, see the fourth sword beginning to manifest. This is a sword of platinum pale blue, shimmering and shining like moonlight. Place the sword before you. Sit back and pause:

"I call upon the power of harmony and peace. I call upon the sword to still my thoughts and heart, to open my mind that I may see with clarity and know. I call upon the sword to keep me in this space so that I may not be disturbed by the illusions and tricks of darkness but remain still inside myself."

73

Turn, finally, to the open point between the sword of water and the sword of spirit. See the fifth sword beginning to manifest before you. See the sword forming in your hands. It is of an opalescent light. Place the sword in front of you and sit back:

"I call upon the sword of innocence, the sword of purity, the sword of the inner child, the sword of wonder. Open my eyes, that I may see the wonder, the purity, the innocence and the truth of the world in which I live, as a child does, and through this innocence and wonder, I may be connected to the magic that exists within myself, and that has come from the Divine, that will keep me safe, as I wake and dream."

Turn your body back to face the sword of spirit, the first sword that was planted. Hold up your left hand and visualise an eleventh sword with the blade pointing down into the deep earth on which you sit. This is the sword of your guardian angel who watches over you at all times and keeps you safe. Imagine it vividly in your mind. This sword is forged of the same colour as your guardian angel's wings:

"I call upon the power of my guardian angel. I call upon the power of his sword, to keep me safe, to guide my steps along the path, to keep me protected and well, as I wake and dream."

Hold out your right hand and visualise the twelfth and final sword. Its blade is pointing deep into the earth. This is your own sword, forged from the light of your very own soul, shimmering and shining with your own unique magic:

"Finally, I call upon the power of my own sword, the sword forged from the light of my soul. My soul is the part of me that is divine and joined with God. This sword completes the eleven that have gone before it and makes twelve. Twelve holy swords to keep me safe and well, to guide me on the path and keep me free from darkness, to keep me well, as I wake and dream."

See in your mind the swords form a sphere of light around you, each one of the swords contributing its own unique glow and hue. The field of force around you is strong and pulsates with multicoloured power. You are safe and protected inside its light.

If you wish to allow this visualisation to become more mobile and instantly accessible, then you can visualise that the field of light draws closer to your body until it takes the shape of an impenetrable armour or you can shrink the sphere of light to surround you like a cocoon or egg.

In times when you feel threatened by the darkness, simply see yourself standing within twelve swords of light, with a sword at either hand and know that you are safe and protected, guarded and well.

Indeed, this visualisation is complex and, as I said, you may find it difficult to master at first, but visualisations are no less powerful for words read out of a book or a ritual followed step by step. If the intent and the desire exist the technique will follow.

Protection is important in the world in which we live. As the light grows, the darkness does also. We are approaching an important time in which the evolution of mankind will be tested and tried to its extreme. Protection becomes more and more important as we draw closer to the portal of order that will lead to paradise and bliss. Begin to take responsibility for your life. Call upon your guides and guardians but also play your part and invoke the protection that is required to keep you safe on the path of light that you tread. Know that the Masters watch and protect you as they can and that their love is always with you.

Know also that their joy and their happiness follows those who make efforts to safeguard and guide themselves.

This visualisation can be placed and dedicated into a crystal or a pendant that is worn around the neck, fashioned into the image of a sword, in gold or silver. The circle of swords can be drawn onto a piece of paper and stuffed into a wallet or pocket where it can be instantly referred to in times of need to strengthen the visualisation that already exists inside your mind. By anointing yourself with frankincense, sage and lavender oil, you will surround yourself with a powerful, protective energy field but, ultimately, it is your own desire to keep yourself safe and your knowledge to know that you cannot be harmed, that is the ultimate protection.

Go then in peace and love, spiritual warriors of the future, champions of the light. Bring order to chaos and peace to disharmony.

KWAN YIN

The Ritual of Compassion

I am Kwan Yin, Lady Ascended Master, Lady of Shambhala, Patroness of Compassion and Peace, Bringer of Order and Stillness, Custodian of Rest and Healing Light.

I carry the pearl-white flame of compassion, a flame which once knew physical manifestation upon the earth in those sacred spaces and temples which were dedicated to and overseen by my presence and power; a physical manifestation and representation of the compassion of mankind for mankind; the ability to be moved through joy and sadness, through love, and a deep and sincere empathy for the suffering of others; a power of generosity and sacrifice which allows one to give to another, in all beauty, the unconditional nature of love.

For a long time, mankind has misunderstood what compassion really means and has replaced it with pity and charity. Compassion has become a word almost unused in the vocabulary of many men and women, it has become an almost abstract and quite bizarre concept.

Compassion is an empathy for the plight of the world and all those who live upon it. It is a sensitivity to the needs and requirements of those who surround you in your atmosphere and environment. It is an understanding which exists deep within the heart of those who are less fortunate and in more need than yourself. It is akin to the mother's sensitivity for her child. It is akin to the earth's sensitivity for its children, the plants and the animals of the world. It is the gift which I retain and remember. It is my offering and my gift back to mankind, in order to heal the wound of anger, envy, bitterness and revenge. For, once compassion burns brightly in the heart, then alongside arrives serenity and peace, and when one is serene then one transcends the need to indulge in the panic and chaos of the world and one carries the ability to perceive the reality in which one lives from the lofty perspective of the observer, as well as the lowly perspective of the participator.

Compassion, therefore, brings peace, serenity, stillness, love, beauty, wonder, joy and healing. Serenity is one of the keys to the future. Compassion is a route which can be taken to reach it.

The ritual which I offer is a simple ritual of compassion and healing. It can be used to heal yourself or to heal another. It can be used time and time again to increase, strengthen and to further understand the existence of compassion inside the heart.

Prepare yourself by bathing in water which has had drops of Neroli oil added to it. Relax in this aroma and allow your mind to enter into a deep state of rest and calm. Having done this, dress in a garment of white or pale pink and enter into your ritual space.

Light a pale pink candle and sit before its light, resting and breathing gently and calmly. Draw my symbol into the air to invoke my energy.

Having gathered around you those things which you feel inspire compassion inside yourself, images of friends, members of family, images of animals, scenery, sadness, joy, poetry and musical objects and art, allow yourself to slowly begin to explore these images and pictures one by one, sensing and seeing them not only with your eyes and your hands but also with your heart. Explore the full depth of that which you feel to be compassion, experiencing the emotion and allowing it to grow and swell and fill you with its power, until you are warm and buzzing with strength.

Once you feel the flame of compassion burning in your heart, close your eyes and focus in upon it. Place your hands over the heart centre and feel the strength of its light. Gently begin to rock the body in a spiralling, slow-turning motion and hum to the sound of the music which you play, focusing, with your eyes closed, upon the power of your own love which you have generated inside yourself through the act of emotional evocation, through the compassion that you have found and conjured within.

If you now choose to use this energy to heal another, then open your eyes and take a photograph or a piece of paper that bears that person's name and stare at it for a few moments, allowing your energy to extend outwards and to make a strong and powerful connection with this person. Feel the radiance and the light of your inner love pouring into the photograph and through the resonance of the image of the name stored thereon towards the person. Hold the image close to your heart and close your eyes again and enter back into the slow, spiralling, rocking rhythm with which you have detached yourself from your body. Hum and listen to the sound of the music.

If you are sending healing to yourself, then keep your hands firmly placed over the heart centre and focus your attention and concentration upon that aspect of your soul, personality or physical being which requires healing. See, in your mind's eye, how the pearl-white flame of compassion begins to glow, to grow, to bloom, to expand until it fills the body, until it surrounds the body with a pearl-white, fiery light. Feel the energy of this flame transforming and energising, reaching out and giving light and life.

When you feel that the energy has passed, place the photograph down upon the floor, take your hands away from your heart and place them at either side of your body. Begin to take slow, deep breaths and allow your consciousness to begin to expand outwards. Listen to the sound of the music and the sounds which go beyond it, the sounds of everyday life, the sounds of the house and the room.

Smell the air and any incense which you may have lit. Feel the light of the candle shining through your eyelids. Relax, expand and feel yourself as a tranquil, calm, peaceful being of light.

Before you conclude this small and simple ritual, imagine that you are sitting in the centre of a white waterlily. It is huge and its petals radiate a luminescent light. With a simple thought, the petals of the lily begin to rise until they form a tight, translucent bubble of light around you. The lily will help keep inside you this feeling of tranquillity and calm, of stillness and peace and will help also to keep away disturbance, pain, heartache and unrest. Once the lily is sealed around you, you can allow the candle to burn down and leave the room to continue with your day.

The photographs, images, poems or music which you used may change as you repeat the ritual or you may keep these same prompts. If you can carry a few of them around with you, they will be an aid throughout your life to create instantaneous moments of compassion or stillness. They will help you enter into a space of serenity when needed, wherever you are or however difficult the situation may be.

By staring at the photo and allowing the flame of compassion to begin to grow and expand within your heart, you will be taken back to when you attuned yourself and touched deep universal peace, strength and calm. You will find yourself anchored, earthed and rooted through this love.

Compassion is like a radiating, contagious symptom of light. You will find that if you live your life within it, you will spread it through the example of your being. The more compassion you show to others, the more compassion they will show to you and you will enter into a wonderful state of bliss, serenity and peace.

Try to exercise compassion in your life, to look at the people who surround you and not to judge them, not to despise them, not to envy them or hate them, but to love them and to allow that love to become a channel through you, in the manner in which you treat them and talk of them, allowing yourself to demonstrate and express the creative energy of your compassion, of your beauty.

Keep time and space to make love to others in art forms which you excel at and allow your sensitivity to those around you to expand so much that you can feel them, almost as if they were part of your very own being, extentions of your character and personality.

Healing is, in a sense, love, and illness is a lack of it, but the lack of love exists in the soul, in the heart, in the mind or in the body. It is a need for energy which does not exist physically. It is the energy of love which is limitless, which can nurture, cure, heal and clarify, and which we are all inheritors of; that power to give. Acknowledge this truth and become one with this power.

Go forward in love and light and take this small and simple knowledge with you: compassion is not something which can be created but it is an ability which can be cultivated. It exists inside us all as a small pearl and seed of light.

SAINT GERMAIN

The Ritual of Transformation

Transformation has been spoken about many times. It seems to be the watchword on everybody's lips. It seems to be what everyone is searching for, what everyone is journeying towards, what everyone is indulging in. To some, it is an excuse, to others a dream, to even more it is a way of life. They move through a series of constant transformations which seem to never bring them to the point which they desire, which never bring them to the point of outcome which they are really aiming to achieve. To others it is an art form which eludes them. To more, it is something which does not truly exist for them. There are those who are limited, imprisoned, tethered and tied to their constant lives, never breaking free of their limitations, their routines, their patterns.

In truth, transformation is the ultimate liberation. It is a point where one thing becomes another. It is the pivot of evolution which is found many times within people's lives. People experience transformational moments every day, or at certain points in their lives, which are landmarks in the movement of their life paths and which they do not fully comprehend or understand.

Transformations can be celebrated, acknowledged and even amplified through ritual and ceremony, but, most importantly, through perception, recognition and understanding. Transformation occurs on everybody's birthday, as they move from one age to another; as they adopt the confines and limitations of the new age and relinquish and release all the wonders of the age that has passed, as they move into the liberating factors of their new birth-year, as they become older, more mature and more responsible.

Transformations occur during marriages, during separations, during divorces, during the birth of a child, the death of a child, the death of a loved one, the death of a friend. Transformations occur when people move home, change their career or job. Transformations occur when people encounter the unexpected in their lives which creates difficulty, chaos or harmony and peace. Transformations occur when someone falls in love and transformations occur when someone falls out of it.

Life is full of transformation and, in truth, apart from love, it is the only constant energy which ever exists in the universe. God itself is an energy which is constantly transforming due to the experiences of his children, mankind, which is slowly but surely returning to the Source, carrying with it all the experiences which it has learned on earth and in other dimensions and planets.

Mankind transforms itself constantly from one level of understanding to another. The earth also moves through transformations and all the life forms from one type of species to another.

Transformation then is a thing which can be nurtured, encouraged, celebrated and focused upon. The rituals which I shall detail will provide you with the technique to do this, but also, from time to time, transformation needs help and assistance. We are all prone to moments in our lives where we feel blocked or obstructed by people, situations, circumstances, negative energies, mistakes, problems or incidents. We can overcome them, or transcend them with a little assistance and help from the universe.

By focusing the power of our will and the power of our emotions upon these obstacles, we can convert them into something which can aid us and help us. We can use the power of spiritual alchemy to turn these blockages into their opposites so that they become signposts along our life's path.

Therefore, there are two major rituals which are concerned with the power of transformation, acknowledging and respecting transformations which have occurred within our life and helping transformations to occur. To begin with, however, we need to have perception. Perception is the foundation stone of transformation. It is the beginning point of acknowledging and recognising transformation in our lives and also of acknowledging and recognising the need for transformation. Perception is a state of consciousness, a state of mental understanding. It is realisation of need or realisation of the evidence of something which already exists.

In order to be perceptually aware, we must open our eyes, the inner eye also, to the portents and omens which the universe will provide us with. We must also open our ears to the words which will ensue from the mouths of others and also from our own. We must listen to the sound of the wind, to see if any words are carried within its whispers; the sounds of the rustling of the trees; the songs of the birds; the gentle gurgle of the river and the stream. We must also open our hearts and feel the different sensations which are emanating from other people or from the Anima Mundi, the spirit of the world.

In times of confusion and chaos where nothing seems to be moving or flowing, we, ourselves, must become like our surroundings, still, tranquil, calm and peaceful. If we allow ourselves to become impatient, agitated and irritated, then we cannot attune ourselves to our environment and locate the blockage which places us at a standstill. By attuning ourselves to the stillness of our environment, the blockage which stands in our way will become obvious, either shown to us as a vision or given to us as knowledge, or provided to us in a symbolic manner through something which we shall see or experience in a place or with a person. By attuning ourselves to the stillness, the blockage will become evident and obvious and then we can go about creating a way of transforming it.

Here follows then two rituals, simple and yet powerful. They must be used only when you feel deep within your heart that it is appropriate to do so. Because of the nature of these rituals and the powers which they call upon, they should not be used glibly. You must take full responsibility for all the works which you create upon the earth, whether they are works of hand, heart, mind or soul. Energy which you place into achieving something, even if it is only on an energy level, is an energy which will return to you threefold.

This is the ancient universal law and, therefore, if you are placing your energy and your effort into transforming a situation, you must be sure that it is a transformation or situation which has not been placed before you in order for you to learn something but in order, instead, for you to transcend it. You must use your inner knowledge, your intuition, and most of all, your honesty and truth.

The first ritual

For the ritual concerned with acknowledging transformational situations which occur within your life, you will need only one violet candle. Light the violet candle and sit before it. Calm and still yourself, relax. Then take a few moments to meditate.

Using the candle's light, allow your thoughts to wander to the thing in your life which you are going to acknowledge or celebrate. Explore this thing with the fullness of your emotions and your mental focus. If it is a sad situation, then do not be frightened of allowing the tears to fall. If it is a joyous one, then do not be afraid to smile or laugh.

Once your thoughts and your heart, and most importantly your energy, are focused upon the situation of acknowledgement, take the symbol which you have chosen to represent this thing, and place it beneath the candle so that it rests in the candle's pool of light.

If you are celebrating, for instance, an engagement or marriage, then place an engagement ring or a wedding ring beneath the candle, combined with a photo of the person who you are to be joined with. If you are acknowledging the passing of a loved one or the breaking of a relationship or marriage, then place a photograph or an item which is connected with them on an energetic level, a piece of their belongings, in the candle's light. If you are acknowledging a transition of age, then place a photo of yourself or the person whose birthday it will be, beneath the candle. If you are acknowledging a birth, then place something which has been bought for the unborn child, or a list of names, or an early foetal photograph of the child, beneath the candle. Take a few moments to allow yourself to respond emotionally to these objects. Touch and hold them, caress and acknowledge them.

Now draw the symbol which is connected to myself, the hectogram (a seven pointed star standing on two feet). Draw it with the right hand, imagining that you are drawing the energy in the air, with the palm of the hand. See in your mind the hectogram drawn in violet light, in violet fire. This is the symbol which will draw my energy to you and attune your space to my space. Call upon me by name in this fashion:

"I call upon the presence and the power of Saint Germain, Lord and Master of the violet flame; Patron of transformation and spiritual alchemy. May your presence be drawn to my presence and enter into this space which I have created in order that you may oversee, guide, bless and protect me in this ritual of acknowledgement and recognition."

Then talk about the situation which you are acknowledging and recognising. Talk as if you were talking to a friend or a loved one, explaining it in minute detail. Try to place as much emotion into this as you possibly can. Talk about the people. Describe them.

If you are talking about a loved one, someone you are joining to, someone who is experiencing a birth, then talk about the positive aspects of them. Fill your description with light and joy. If you are talking about someone who has passed over, then do not be frightened to become tearful and emotional. If you are talking about yourself, be positive and constructive. Do not be frightened to let your ego fly a little in the description.

Detail, strongly and securely, the point of acknowledgement. Say that you recognise and realise that this is a time of transformation and ask for guidance. Ask that you will be shown the way. Ask that you will be made to realise all the positive and the negative situations which will occur from the transformation and ask that you will be given the wisdom to weather them and work with them in a positive and creative fashion.

Then say this prayer whilst visualising the hectogram before you and visualising the violet flame surrounding the object and then yourself:

"All things must change. This is the law of the universe. Nothing can remain static and everything moves eternally onwards. Even when there is stillness, there is still constant

movement which can sometimes neither be seen nor felt, and even when my life feels as if it is moving nowhere, there is always progression and evolution.

I acknowledge this event as a powerful moment of transformation in my life. I acknowledge that I will never be the same again and ask for guidance, grace, blessing, protection, love and understanding as I step forward upon this path, into my new life, into this new realm.

I have acknowledged and seen this moment. Fill me now with the guidance to make this progression a good one. Reward me with understanding for my perception by the grace of God, the Source, the one light from which all life came, by your grace, Saint Germain, and the power of the violet flame. Allow this then to be so."

See in your mind moments of the past and see the present situation which causes it to change. See the present burnt and consumed by the violet flame and allow the future to form where the present once was. Allow the violet flame to give you whatever you need, strength, courage, power, protection, love and guidance. Open your mind and your heart to that which you wish to receive and allow yourself to step into this power and this energy.

Once this has been done, allow the candle to burn down, setting it somewhere in your room where your eye will wander upon it from time to time. Each time you see it, acknowledge and recognise that, as the candle burns, transforming itself and eventually transforming its light into nothingness, that it is a symbol of a constant transformation or cycle of your life now, as you have chosen, to consciously move into the new transformational cycle of your existence.

Also, it is important to do something for yourself which will be a physical, external manifestation of the transformation which has occurred. This could be an object which you will purchase or make. It could be something which you will do, something that you will construct. It could be an action: the writing of a letter, making a phone call, taking a journey. It is important, to make a strong, physical action which appears to the conscious and the subconscious mind, which underlines and strengthens the acknowledgement of the transformation which you have just seen and recognised.

It is important also to understand that there is no turning back and that once you have acknowledged the transformation which has occurred within your life and stepped boldly forward, you can no longer deny it and you must surrender to the grace of the flame.

Try to remain open to, and aware of, any dreams or visions which you may have concerning this transformation, which may be given as guidance, in meditations, or times during the day when you are relaxed. Also, stay aware of the words which may be spoken by others, or universal indications and hints which may be provided to you, throughout your daily experiences. Remain open and in a state of awareness and you may be given guidance to help you with the transition which will occur.

The second ritual

You will need to construct the sacred space as mentioned before in however complicated or simple fashion. Gather together the things which you will need for the ritual and make sure that your space is secure.

For this ritual you will need seven violet candles, which you have previously anointed with lavender oil, making sure that you anoint the candles with a downwards sweep from the wick to the base of the candle's stem. Place the candles in candle holders and light them.

Sit before them, relax, make yourself comfortable within your space and centre yourself. Focus for a short time upon that thing which you would desire to be transformed: a situation, an obstacle, a lack of something, an abundance of something, the attitude of a person, a person themselves, an attitude which exists within your own consciousness or your own heart, any form of situation which is causing a blockage in the forward movement on your path.

Take a blank piece of paper and a pencil or pen and begin to write down vividly the blockage which you have become aware of. Do not write down how you would like to have this blockage transformed. If you provide too many specific details, then the energy of the universe will be expended before the completion of the transformation has occurred.

It is important to give the universe a free hand on how it will deal with the transformation. Universal energy works economically and the universe will find the simplest and yet most effective way of dealing with your request. When you have completed writing down on the piece of paper that which you would desire to be transformed, write at the bottom of the page :

"To harm none, for the good of all, and in accordance with the Divine Will, allow this then to be transformed and changed, providing me with forward movement on my life's path, purpose and task."

Hold the paper in your hand and read what you have written out loud as if you were addressing it to the candles themselves. When you have finished, draw over the piece of paper my symbol, the hectogram, with the right hand, as if you were drawing the image with the palm, visualising the hectogram being drawn with a violet fire.

Fold the piece of paper and place it into a metal bowl or dish which you have already prepared. You may need to place this dish on a tile of wood or clay which will protect the floor from heat. Now light the paper and, as the paper burns, throw some loose lavender into the fire's flames. Repeat this invocation and prayer as the paper burns:

> *"Transformed by fire, and cleansed by the power of this laven-*
> *der, words which I have written, follow the stream and energy*
> *of my thoughts and feelings, and be transformed. Liberate me,*
> *Violet Flame, and assist in this liberation, Saint Germain,*
> *Patron of spiritual alchemy and transformation.*
>
> *Aid me in releasing those things which I consciously or sub-*
> *consciously hold on to, for I know that I have learnt the lesson*
> *of this obstacle and now need only to transcend it with my*
> *thoughts and heart in order to move forward into the next*
> *stage of experience in my life.*
>
> *Burn them away and, as they burn, sever the ties which exist*
> *between me and them and transform them so that they may be*
> *returned to me as blessings, signs, guidance and assistance*
> *upon my path.*
>
> *Allow this to be done in the name of love and light, in the*
> *name of peace and harmony and in the name of spiritual evo-*
> *lution, as long as this flows in accordance with the universe's*
> *will, harms none and is for the good of all. Allow this then to*
> *be so. So mote it be. Amen."*

Allow the fire to burn the paper completely until only ashes are left. Spend a few moments focusing on the light of the candles again and seeing in your mind's eye the situation which you would have transformed burnt away by violet fire.

Leave the seven violet flames to burn the candles down completely, making sure that this has been done safely and so that the candles are in view, in order to remind your conscious and deep subconscious minds that the transformation is in process.

Also, take the ashes of the burnt paper, and bury them in the earth to ensure that the transformation will occur upon a physical level.

Try not to focus too much thought upon the nature of the transformation which you have set in motion otherwise you will be consciously and subconsciously making demands upon the universe's energy and the manner in which the universe operates and this will place strain upon the success of the ritual.

If you find your thoughts wandering in this direction, remove them from this area immediately and do not allow yourself to dwell upon this, calling back the energy of the ritual itself. Instead, release the power completely and allow the transformation to occur naturally within your life.

It is important to perform the first ritual of acknowledgement, if at all possible, on a full moon. The second ritual should take place when the moon is waxing. If the ritual is a complete banishment rather than a transformation, it should be performed when the moon is waning. Rituals should never be performed when the moon is dark.

Rituals and transformations are extremely powerful and it is important to be cautious, before you take the step of instigating a ritual. Make sure that the ritual will not cause the free will of any individual to be harmed or tampered with. Although the energy is monitored by my presence and the power of the violet flame, some of your personal energy is involved in the ritual and if you desire to interfere with anybody's free will, then you will be invoking a negative return of energy which may make your life difficult and troublesome.

It is important, therefore, for you to remember what I said earlier about the importance of rituals; their power, and the importance of neither taking them lightly nor performing them without a great deal of consideration and forethought.

The power of rituals of transformation has been tried and tested throughout the centuries. To experience the transformation will convince you of their power and provide you with the necessary understanding of the caution needed for your work.

Transformation is a constant process. The acknowledgement of it is something which has been lost from mankind and the working of transformation is something which mankind has forgotten or renounced performing a long time ago.

Indulging in rituals and transformation, or the acknowledgement of transformation, is for mankind a step closer to re-entering into the fullness of its power and to draw to them their divine inheritance as co-creators of its reality upon the earth.

Use that part of you which is divine and acknowledge that you have the power to create and recreate the reality in which you live, through the power of divine alchemy and spiritual transformation.

LADY NADA

The Ritual of Joy

Joy is something which is little understood in the modern world in which we live. Yet in truth, joy was one of the primary purposes of life, one of the main reasons why God, the Source, the Divine Origin of all life, created mankind.

Joy is not a complicated emotion or pleasure, it is simple and childlike. Joy does not have to be bought through complicated and witty comedy, through great gifts or presents, through immense and overpowering experiences, but joy can be found in the simplicity of a growing flower or the wonder of a clear summer's day, or the love of a child or a friend.

Joy is often at its most potent when it is found in the simplest of places and caused by the simplest of experiences. Joy, caused artificially, through great and generous celebration and expense, and through demonstration in order to impress and gratify, is often shallow and fruitless, and two-dimensional. It is often wasted because it does not touch the heart as plain wonder does.

If you have forgotten what joy is like, if you feel that your life has been so dark and dim that you can no longer even recall the taste of joy within your life, then you should take yourself to the side of a child and watch them play, for joy is in the constant and ever present moment of a child's life.

It is the joy of a toy which the child loves and plays with, the joy of food at dinner time, the joy of grass beneath bare feet, the joy of water on a hot summer's day, the joy of ice-cream and chocolate; the sweet pleasures of life which fill a child's face with radiance and happiness, which transcend the artificial pleasures which we have come to look upon as our life.

It is through the eyes of children that we can re-learn the truth behind happiness, that we can reach out again with innocent hands and touch the sparkle of existence.

Some feel that the earth is a place devoid of joy but this is not so. Even those in their darkest hours and their most unpleasant predicaments experience joy at some point in their lives.

There is no moment so dark, no experience so wretched, no evil so glum, that it has the power to extinguish joy within the heart of any human being; for as long as you live, no matter what you have experienced or who you have lost, no matter what you have lost, or what you have seen, you always have something to be joyous about.

For example, life itself, which forces your heart to beat, the prospect of a future, the chance to make things better or to heal that which has been wounded, whether it is another person or yourself, the opportunity to start again.

Some people feel that joy is a sin and that the only route or path to spirituality is through self-deprivation: by not focusing the eyes, the ears, the senses, upon the path of light and by ignoring laughter and happiness. The over-serious nature of those who seek enlightenment in this manner kills the spark within themselves which is divine and which is their only chance of finding the way.

Those who constantly carry a little of the child inside themselves, a little innocence, a little wonder, a little happiness, those are the ones who will find the true path which leads to understanding.

Those are the ones who will be guided through the gateways into paradise again, back to the Garden of Eden where man began. For happiness, laughter and joy are forces of light which raise consciousness, which expand vibration, which enable you to realign yourself once again with that part of you which is divine and, through resonance, realign with God. For God is not a being devoid of happiness but one who consists of it.

Therefore, we must not become so over-serious as to forget to smile or laugh, for the greatest teaching and the greatest learning can be done in an atmosphere of happiness and laughter, and the strongest healing takes place when the patient once again learns how to smile and feels love inside their heart. No healing and no awakening can take place in shadow which is devoid of light, for light is love and light is laughter and light is joy.

Some people feel that, through the experiences which they have had and the mistakes which they have made, they have lost the right to experience joy or forgotten how to find it, or how to encourage it to grow inside their hearts. They feel that all that is left inside is misery and pain, sorrow and sadness and, because of this, they begin to shrink and die and they fade away into the background, undoing, uncreating themselves, making themselves once again plain and invisible.

But as long as you live, there exists inside yourself the seed, the potential, the power to laugh and to smile, and if you have grown unaccustomed to this energy and this presence in your life, then you must not wait for it to find you but you must seek it out.

You must think of those people and those places, those experiences in your past dim and distant life which brought you happiness and you must retrace your steps to experience these things again: to skate upon the ice, to kick a ball upon the grass with children, captivated and consumed by the moment of the game, to write poetry in the sunshine or sleep by the sound of a babbling brook, to laugh with friends, to joke with jokers, to experience the rushing, gurgling and giggling wonder of happiness, brought about by anyone or anything: through decadence, through luxury, through moments spent with good and sincere friends laughing about the world.

Joy is the greatest alchemist and has the power to transform darkness into light. Through laughter, serious and intense moments can be transformed. Energy which is blocked can be released and a movement can proceed.

People who are plummeting into spirals of despair can raise themselves to the heights of happiness. Serious matters which could cause disaster and destruction can be transformed into moments of mutual laughter. Tensions can be released and bubbles burst, and wonders and miracles achieved.

Joy is a force which binds and joins people together, which liberates them and frees them. It is not a power that victimises or excludes or isolates. It is not a form of amusement based on prejudice. It is not banal and frivolous silliness. It is a warm, gathering energy which joins and connects, which gives people hope, which gives people life.

Find for yourself then those things which make you laugh, seek out a child who is not yet grown so old that they have become consumed by the shadows of scepticism or disappointed by life. Take yourself to the company of those who can still smile at the world and see the beauty, even in its shadows, and allow their light to set you ablaze with your own inner luminescence.

Here follows a ritual of joy which will enable you to open yourself up, in order to create an abundant space where joy may re-enter into your life. It is a ritual of release and acceptance. It is a simple release, a simple ritual, a simple wonder which we are about to invite into our lives:

Bathe yourself in water of rosemary and geranium. Allow the water to wash away all the dirt which is carried on all levels of your being. Allow yourself to float and bathe. Allow yourself to let go of sadness and darkness. Put aside, for just this moment in time, all worries and pains, all concerns and fears.

Dry yourself and enter into the sacred space which you have prepared. Having placed on your altar or table one pale pink candle, light it and trace my symbol in the air above it, then sit back and rest a while.

Here is the prayer that will allow you to enter into the state of grace which will bring joy back into your life:

"Lady Nada, Mary Magdalene, Lady of Shambhala and Lady Ascended Master of Joy and Laughter, open my soul and release the sadness and the sorrow which I carry inside. Pour it onto the earth like a dark offering so that it may be taken from me and transformed into light. Fill the space inside me with happiness and wonder, with all the joys of life which I deserve and need, and all the love of life that I can drink and eat.

For I am a child of the Divine and I was created by God to live in joy, and in my sorrow I do the Divine a disservice by staying within the shadow of that which was meant to be mine. And so I seek and desire assistance and help, to crawl from the shadow into the light and to live my life as it should be: a joyous and celebratory one.

Fill my heart with love and light and seal it tight inside. Gently bring your subtle power to earth and kiss the sweetest kiss upon my lips. Let it signify the beginning of my journey into laughter and happiness."

Now sip the wine or water which you have poured for yourself and eat a little of the bread. Imagine that these are physical representations of the joy which you are consuming and filling yourself with.

Take a flower from the vase that sits by the side of your pale pink candle and pluck the petals until they form a small pile before you.

Now read the prayer a second time. As you speak it, take the petals and allow them to gently fall about your body and your head. Breathe their scents and allow their inner light to enter into your inner being. The petals are the representation and symbol of the unconditional giving energy of God which showers down upon you as a blessing.

As you sit, try to focus upon those aspects of your life which have brought you joy. Immerse yourself in those memories and allow them to make you smile and laugh. Before you close the ritual, decide upon three things that you will do within the next days which will bring you happiness; whether it is talking to a friend, buying something for yourself or doing something which you have not done for a very long time, something which brings you back to happiness inside. Having decided upon these three things, swear and promise to yourself that you will do them.

Close the ritual by ringing a small bell three times. As the last bell sounds, say this:

'Three bells have tolled and they tell the story of the life which lies ahead: a life of laughter and love, a life of joy and smiles, as God intended it to be. This is my promise and I know that the universe will aid me, as long as I aid myself, in finding the happiness which I have lost and bring it back into my heart.

This, then, is my desire. Allow this then to be so, for the good of all and to the harm of none. So mote it be. Amen."

Allow the candle to burn down completely. Allow its light to soothe you to sleep and when you awaken the next day, know that this is the first day of a joyous life watched over by the ever-loving eye of God.

DJWAL KHUL

The Ritual of Serenity

I n these times of chaos and confusion, serenity is to be seen as a precious gift, a precious jewel, a precious treasure. It is a concept, a state of mind, which many have no true perception of.

They have been born into a world which is rife with chaos and disorder, which is rife with destruction, confusion, stress, tension, pain and demand, a life which offers neither serenity nor peace and provides them with no instruction of how to find it for themselves.

Often, those born into this storm, into this melee, find serenity when fate allows them to wonder about the confusion and discomfort. They are like those people who have been born at sea and who have become so used to the rhythm of the waves upon the hull of the ship that, when eventually they find dry land, the stillness of the earth beneath their feet makes them sick.

These children of chaos have become so accustomed to the darkness of this confusion that when they are presented with the light of normality which is serenity and peace, they do not understand it and they cannot endure it or find comfort in its calm.

Therefore, as well as finding serenity for ourselves to retreat to, when life and the circumstances of life batter at our door and make it difficult for us to live and exist, we must also be the teachers of tomorrow's children and educate each and every one of them to the value of serenity, stillness and peace, and signpost the way for them in order that they may be guided towards it and assured that it is indeed real.

Serenity, as well as being a state of mind, is very much a state of heart. It is a mode of being, a concept of behaviour, which is achieved through direct communion with the Divine.

When we are aligned to our Higher Self and through the Higher Self to God, we find in our centre this stillness and peace which is God, which is our self. We achieve this inner calm through our own destiny and fate and by God's will, and no situation, no person or place can move us from the centre of our stillness because we know in these all too few moments of illumination that the universe is indeed perfect and that everything which occurs around us, however violent or distressing, is meant to be; is ordained and flows in accordance with the Divine Source's will.

Serenity then is a retreating into a part of the self whereby a connection can be made to our own higher faculties and capabilities; whereby we can release all the stresses and the trials and tribulations of our mundane reality, giving all our worries and our problems to God and falling back in grace and allowing the Divine to nurture and feed us and provide us with all the guidance, wisdom and power which we require, to move through the different initiations and transformational cycles of our life.

Serenity is many different things to different people, but all these things are tied by a common thread and that thread is inspiration. For some, serenity and alignment to God can come through meditation, to others by listening to music, to others by tending the garden, to others by walking, running, swimming or playing a musical instrument.

Many different ways can be utilised in order for serenity to be found. Each individual who pursues this path of calm is indeed an individual aspect or flicker of the Divine Original Light. Therefore, it is important not to judge or criticise another person's perception of serenity, calm, stillness, peace or the path which they take to achieve it, but to accept and acknowledge this diversity as indeed a divine quality, and to be grateful and thankful for its existence.

The ritual which I shall shortly dictate is not like those rituals which have gone before. It is a ritual which can be modified in accordance with each individual's path to serenity and stillness.

Before I dictate this ritual, I shall speak a little further of the importance of serenity in accordance with our surroundings and those people who orbit us in our lives.

Serenity is a precious and important inner state for ourselves, providing us with communion and attunement to the Divine, providing us with peace, stillness and harmony; emptying and clearing our minds, in order that our thought processes may be sharper and clearer; unloading our heart from unnecessary emotional baggage, in order that it can vibrate out and receive inwards divine, unconditional loving energy, emitted from the Source, which is God.

But there is also a benefit which exists through serenity which is not only for ourselves but for those people close to us and the environment in which we spend our time.

Serenity is to be imagined as a tangible force similar to the scent of a flower. When we ourselves have found serenity, we exude or radiate this tangible energy which can be sensed consciously or unconsciously by those around us.

When someone enters into a room which is full of flowers, instantaneously the smell is noted and uplifts the soul and spirit with its beauty and its wonder. The same can be said of the vibration of serenity, which is emitted by those people who have found and sustained serenity, calm, peace and harmony in their own lives. Around these people, this energy can be sensed and found, and inspires the person who has become sensitive to this force of light to assimilate, adopt and emulate this pattern of thought and behaviour.

Serenity, therefore, is contagious and, through this benign infection, can enable the world to be a clearer and more positive place. Serenity affects our environment by settling upon the objects which surround us. The energy settles upon material things: furniture, textiles, upon all forms of metal, glass and stone, imbuing or filling these objects with serenity and peace.

Therefore, long after we have left these places, the field of serenity which we have exuded and created will remain behind us like an invisible trail or force, and those people who enter into it will feel its beneficial effects as it calms, soothes and stills them.

A group of people who have found serenity can often combine the serenity field which they emanate, focusing it towards individuals, places or situations where serenity is needed and necessary. This can dampen angry, frightened, jealous or envious people, reducing a potentially riotous crowd into a peaceful gathering.

It can be sent to places in the world which are scarred by war or it can be sent to places where people need rest such as hospitals and homes for those who need special care.

If you yourself find, with the aid of this ritual, the small still place inside yourself known as serenity, then teach and pass on this precious gift to others and then, together, align and focus the power of your thoughts and hearts in order that you may pass this power on to those in great need.

In order to perform this ritual, you will need to take yourself to a place which inspires you and provides you with a sense of serenity and peace, whether that is your own living room, your garden, a park nearby; a place which brings you happiness or joy, whether it means that you are performing some form of artistic work, are lying upon your bed, are busy tending your flowers or baking in the kitchen, it does not matter. It is only important that you take yourself to that place and that situation which brings you peace and happiness.

As you do these things that inspire you, that bring you this feeling, surrender yourself completely to your own actions. Allow yourself to completely revel in the sensual experience which brings you stillness, serenity and joy. If you feel the need to sing or hum gently to yourself or speak to yourself soothingly, then do so, being not fearful of those people who may hear you in this endeavour.

Completely throw yourself into these tasks which bring you deep serenity and joy, abandon yourself to them, then allow yourself to find the small, still space of calm and peace.

When you have entered into this space, light a white candle. Draw my symbol into the flame and focus your concentration and attention upon your own heart centre. Try to become completely aware of the feeling in your heart; whether it is an emotional feeling, a mental understanding or a physical sensation, bring your attention to this point of your body. Now close your eyes and allow your consciousness, your mind, to travel into your heart.

Most people imagine that their consciousness is located between the eyebrows, where the brow centre or third eye is actually found. If this is the same for you, then imagine your consciousness as a small glowing ball of light which now begins to descend down your throat, the upper part of your chest and into the heart centre itself.

Feel yourself travelling like a ball of living light energy into the centre of your own heart which glows and shines with a green and pink light, the colour of the heart chakra. Go deeper in a slow, spiralling fashion, deep into the core of the heart itself. Imagine, as you enter this portal of peace that you find, that the core of your own heart is a pearl of brilliant white light.

Enter into the pearl and feel its radiance, its illumination, filling every part of your body and being. Now allow the pearl to force your consciousness to rise like a rocket, rising out of the heart centre, up through the top part of the chest, which you journeyed down previously, through the throat, up into the face, past the mouth, nose and brow, up to the top of the head and out through the crown of the head, high into the air above you.

Allow yourself to be blown out, shot like a rocket from your own physical body high into the air, higher and higher and higher. After a short time, you will arrive at a white space which will consist of brilliant white light, all-consuming, still as white as snow.

This is your God-Self, your Divine Being, your Higher Self, the part of you which remains in those other dimensional realities, which you return to after the end of physical life. It is the part of you which remains connected to God.

Relax and surrender to this whiteness. Allow it, if you will, to speak to you or to show you images, or simply to provide you with power and strength. Abandon yourself completely to whatever you may experience here but, most importantly, focus upon this place's strength, serenity and peace.

You may find that this place takes on a shape or form which reminds you of a beautiful place which you have been to or heard about in your life. If this is so, then enjoy that place for itself. You may find that you are prompted to place questions to the white light and that the questions are even answered as thoughts which appear in your mind or images which you perceive. This is also good and indicates a healthy communication and connection to the Higher or Divine Self; or you may find that you simply rest here in the white space, fed by its nurturing brilliance.

After some time, your consciousness will begin to return, flowing down the shaft of light which enters the crown through the top of the head, passing down past the brow, nose, mouth, through the throat, moving on down through the top part of the chest and returning to the heart. Once again, you will become aware of the centre of the heart, like a brilliant white pearl and its outer surround of pale pink and pale green.

Return to your consciousness, back into its origin between the eyebrows, taking a little of the serenity, peace, power, strength, illumination and knowledge which you have gained from your Higher Self back with you as you re-enter into the conscious reality.

It is, of course, important, before you begin this visualisation, to make sure that you will not be disturbed and that, if you are outside or if you are doing something which causes you to use a fine motor skill, that you are sitting down, your environment is safe and secure, and that you yourself are warm and prepared for any eventuality. If you find any discomfort with any part of this visualisation or exercise, then simply open your eyes to disconnect yourself from the Higher Divine Being and re-centre yourself into your physical form, and no harm will befall you.

This visualisation is a simple way of accentuating and increasing the process of already discovered serenity, taking it to a fine art whereby serenity can be used, not only to strengthen and nurture us, but also to provide us with clear guidance, clear information and clear truths, unfettered by social conditioning and subconscious pressures that originate from our normal waking world.

This process of discovering serenity is extremely important and, in truth, it is only the beginning, the first stepping stone to opening up a whole new dimension of peace and beauty for you, but it is indeed a valid and important movement.

Remember, finding serenity always takes place through inspiration and sensuality to the inspiration, and then leads to the discovery and the remembrance of God.

Go forth then and enter into your own peace, keeping love in your hearts and truth in your minds, embracing the light of tomorrow.

WOTTANA

---

*The Ritual
of Connecting with the
Earth*

I it has taken mankind some time to understand and to believe that the earth is a living being with a soul. In ancient times, which have long since gone, many cultures and civilisations knew this one unique truth which modern man has only recently re-discovered after a long period of forgetfulness.

The earth is the mother which nurtures the growth and sustenance of her children, mankind; which provides it with all that is required in order to live and to experience reality: air to breathe and food to eat, water to drink, lands to live upon and explore.

The earth exhibits all the qualities of a mother, providing sustenance, nutrition, love and care for her children, providing them with those things which are needed to help to cure them when they are ill, with those things which can be used to shield them from the harsh elements, with teaching and knowledge, with power and strength.

During the times of mankind's forgetfulness, mankind began to use the materials of the earth in ways which began to cause great destruction and harm to the very fabric of her being. No longer did humans honour her presence, her soul, no longer did they work in accordance with the balance of her rhythms and her life cycles, but they strove to drain the resources which she offered and mutated and warped them in a way which had never been done before. They strove to control the earth and to make it something which it was never meant to be.

Humans have damaged the earth to a point where they stand upon the fringe of self-destruction through their actions. They have damaged the protective skin, consisting of the earth's atmosphere, and they have caused some plants to be completely destroyed so that they will never ever grow again upon the earth.

Even to this day, they continue to lay waste to thousands upon thousands of streams, distressing and harming the ecological environment of the earth, creating imbalance and disharmony, and dancing with the devil on the brink of annihilation. But the earth is more than soil and plants. It is more than herbs and flowers. It is more than chemicals and nutrients. The earth has a soul, a consciousness, a life force which is present in every blade of grass, in every petal of every flower, in every tree, in every field, in every stone, in every drop of water which exists. It is a life force which permeates the planet with an invisible auric energy.

This consciousness of the mother can be reached out to and contacted in order that mankind can, once again, begin to re-establish communion with the mother, live in harmony with the resonance and energy, with the feminine planet's power, learn to tap into the secret knowledge of the goddess, learn how to heal the world and mankind's connection to the divine nurturer, to the creatrix of life.

The earth is not a fragile thing, not a paper lantern which is on the verge of destruction. It has a great regenerative power which will, in time, heal itself. If mankind, ten years from now, destroys itself in a nuclear holocaust, in a ball of fire and destruction and the earth is laid to waste, its energies will repair itself and it will wait in a dormant state until it has regrouped its own internal power, until it can begin to grow again.

The earth does not desire or require our healing energy focused on it. That is not a necessity, it is not something which the earth cannot do without. The earth has the power to transform itself. The earth has the power to rid itself of our presence if it chooses to do so, but the earth has faith in humanity and its soul, and patiently waits, as a mother waits, watching her children grow and hoping that they will not break her heart.

The earth will wait to see what mankind grows into and if mankind destroys itself, in its process of growth, then the earth will regenerate herself and wait for new children to be born. But if mankind can bend its mind back to the understanding and acknowledgement of the consciousness of the planet, then the mother will thrive and grow and reach out with loving arms to re-embrace her children and give them back all the secrets, all the knowledge, all the power which it once shared openly with every man and woman upon the planet and then, and only truly then, will paradise return and harmony and love ensue.

The earth is more than soil, plant and consciousness. It is energy and power: invisible veins of force, meridians called leys which criss-cross the earth in a cradle of power, vortexes, spinning chakras which burn and clean and shine. The earth is a living being which mirrors our own form, our body. It is a storehouse of unlimited power, unlimited understanding and unlimited love. It is an energy which can be attuned to and tapped into in order to manifest reality, in order to soften the harshness of life as we have created it, in order to bring harmony to the seasons and tranquillity to the weather, in order to bring life to the barren areas of existence, in order to create peace and beauty, love and health, harmony and wonder.

The ritual which is given is a ritual of attunement and communion. Once attunement and communion with the earth are achieved, then all things are possible: communion with all life forms upon the planet and attunement to all living things.

Once this unlimited power can be tapped and the consciousness of the earth shared, understanding and energy can be released to provide us with insight. The use of herbal medicine, the use of creating organic gardens, which will joyously surrender powerful fruits and vegetables, which will carry great strength, great healing properties, great universal life forces, which will aid in expanding the consciousness even further and connecting it to the elemental existence of the etheric kingdoms of the planet.

Once communion is achieved, harmony with the earth can be indulged in and the earth will not harm those children whom she loves, but will nourish and protect them and will be seen and understood as a living extension of the personal consciousness, as an external reflection and echo of the inner microcosm of reality. The earth will become the ever-present surrounding mother which she was at the beginning of time.

Although this ritual can be performed indoors, it is more powerful if it is performed outside in the centre of a wood, in a field, by a stream, somewhere that is secluded and quiet and where one is alone.

Walk barefoot upon the land to find your spot, your place, and breathe the air and drink in the rich sun. As you walk, spend time to touch the trees and feel the power which passes through their branches and their trunks.

Hug the trees which you come across, allowing your heart centre to be close to the tree's trunk, opening your consciousness to receive impressions, emotions and images which the tree projects towards your consciousness, to give you guidance, communion and love.

Enter only into those parts of nature where you feel invited, welcomed and encouraged and steer clear of those places which repel or resist you. The earth, like all of us, demands respect and privacy in part and will guide you to the places which are most appropriate for the work at hand.

Smell the flowers and acknowledge the beauty of the grass and, when you have found your place, lie down upon the earth and draw my symbol into the air. Now spread yourself out so that your body becomes a pentagram, the five-pointed star which represents the power of the earth itself.

Lying upon the ground, gaze up at the sky and allow all your thoughts of the mundane world, all your sorrows and discontent, to float into this expanse of blue. With every out-breath, release all your pain, your misery, your confusion, your pessimism, your negativity. Allow the earth to reach out with its invisible arms to embrace you in its gentle loving caress.

Feel yourself connected to the earth, drawn to it by its gravitational mysterious force and power. Feel yourself being sucked into the consciousness of the earth. Feel roots extending from your feet and palms delving deep into the dark soil and umbilical cords of energy joining you with the deep consciousness, the deep current of the planet's light.

Allow your breathing, the pulse of your rhythm and your heart's beat to slow down, and listen to the sound of the beat of the earth, the earth's heart, and join your breathing and your rhythm to it. Close your eyes and relax. Allow your mind to be filled with the knowledge of the goddess. Allow your rhythm to flow in accordance with the rhythm of the earth, as it should and once did. Listen and reach out with your ears and your heart. Reach out with the open space of your mind and allow yourself to be filled with understanding, with power, with strength and communion.

Allow yourself to re-merge with the source of your physical creation. Allow yourself to be drawn back into the darkness of the earth's womb, to reconnect with the source of physical life.

Rest here, safe in this place, attuned and in communion with the power of nature.

When it is time for you to leave, gather yourself together and, before you depart from this sacred space, from this place of interaction with the earth's own consciousness, leave a libation or small sacrifice. Give some grain or tobacco to the earth, the traditional offering, as thanks for this wonderful opportunity and opening into the consciousness of the earth itself. Also, leave a little something of yourself behind: a nail paring, a piece of hair, a few drops of your own blood, a picture of yourself, an object which you value and love. Create a hole in the earth and place this offering there. Bury the offering and step back and say these words:

"Great mother earth, goddess, divine creatrix, mother of life, I leave here an offering of thanks and a piece of myself behind as a promise and as a gift, in the hope that we shall stay joined and connected as one; in the hope that our communion will continue, as it did in the very beginning and as it was always meant to do, in the hope that your consciousness will be joined to mine and I may learn through the experience of its power and love, in the hope that I shall grow as you grow, heal as you heal, know as you know, in the hope that I shall always keep your awareness in my mind no matter where I am, in the hope that we two shall be one again."

Walk slowly back into your life looking for signs, omens and portents along the way. Be aware of the signs which the earth will give you and the guidance of the goddess.

If you perform this ritual at home, then make the libation within your own garden or a space nearby. By lying upon the floor inside the house you can still achieve communion with the spiritual essence of the earth but communion with nature itself is lacking and it is better to perform this ritual outside with the elements.

From this point on, make a conscious effort to acknowledge the power of the earth more fully. Love and honour it, abide by its laws. Make a conscious effort to keep the knowledge that the earth lives in your mind and heart and open yourself to the awareness which the planet can give.

Appendix

QUESTIONS AND ANSWERS

Why should I pray to Ascended Masters or to Angels and not directly to God? Why should I have anyone (like Angels, Masters) between me and God?
Ascended Masters are our brothers and sisters in light, those that have gone before us, human beings once like ourselves. They have become perfected beings through transcendence of limitation and they are aware of their own divinity and are close to God. As intermediaries with the Divine, they can utilise divine power that flows in accordance with God's will to aid us in a more empathic way. They are not alternatives for God or angels but can be seen as a ladder whereby our feelings and needs may reach God more clearly, be understood and answered through their grace from the Creator itself.

Do the Masters need to be worshipped?
The Masters are not beings to be worshipped but friends, teachers, and guides to be worked with. They are our spiritual forefathers and ancestors who have transcended limitation before us and now look back to guide us.

How do I draw the Symbols correctly?
With the palm of the hand (palm chakra), with a wand, a crystal, or with the first two fingers as in the sign for benediction.
There are no fast rules concerning drawing the symbols, they can be big or small, with any part of them drawn in any order, but they must be visualised in colour in order to be fully activated. (See pages 125 and 126 for colours.)

What else can I do with the Symbols?
With the help of the symbols you can easily attune with the consciousness and wisdom of the Masters and ask for blessing, protection, guidance and healing. You can use the Symbols on business cards, on stationery, or as jewellery etc., as long as

they are used privately. However, the symbols are copyrighted against use for commercial purposes but private use is permitted.

Do the moon phases have any influence on the rituals?
Yes. The rituals should be performed, whenever possible, in accordance with the following moon-phases:
- waxing moon: beginnings, starting, birth, creation
- full moon: manifestations, psychic power, becoming
- waning moon: banishing, releasing, tie breaking
- dark moon: rituals should never be performed when the moon is dark

How do I prepare myself for a ritual?
To begin with, it is important to focus upon the creation of your ritual space and this may be as elaborate or as simple as you wish in the construction of this sacred area.
Make sure that you have successfully gathered together all those things which you will need for the ritual and have them placed around you. Take a few moments to settle yourself and make yourself feel comfortable and at home here. Take a few moments to run over in your mind all those things which you will require to perform the ritual; have you secured your space and made sure that you will not be disturbed?
Do you have time afterwards to rest and feel the energies? Some rituals require that you produce something or that you go out to buy something. Please make sure you have enough time for this so you do not need to do these things in a rush because you would lose the serenity which was created in the ritual.

When will the effects of the ritual show?
This depends upon your efforts and if your desire flows in accordance with the divine will, but usually within a month.

Is it dangerous to perform a ritual?
The rituals are overseen by the Ascended Masters but it is a cosmic law that energy follows thought or deed. Only your intent can decide an eventual negative flashback of energy. If you send negative energy purposefully, negative energy will return to you and no protection will help, be it as elaborate as possible. See Master Saint Germain's comments on page 93.

Can I do something wrong which could affect my mental or physical health?
If your intent is clear, no. The Ascended Masters, our brothers and sisters who have gone before us, present these rituals to us so we may fill our lives and our world with light, and create healing, love and compassion for each other.

LIST OF THE REQUIRED ITEMS FOR THE RITUALS

LADY NIGHTINGALE - *The Ritual of Awakening*
One white cloth for the altar, three white candles, photo(s) of loved ones, items (books, crystals, figures) which represent spiritual truths to you, one quartz crystal.

SERAPIS BEY - *The Ritual of Angels*
Frankincense oil, white feathers, white clothes, a white or silver candle, a round or square mirror, frankincense or myrrh, perhaps photos of loved ones.

LADY MIRIAM - *The Rituals of the Seasons*
The Ritual of Spring
Petals of one or more roses, white clothes, a bunch of flowers in a vase, paper and pen, a white candle, a chalice (or simply a beautiful drinking glass), wine or water, bread, flower or vegetable seeds.
The Ritual of Summer
Lemon grass oil, two each of green, red and yellow candles.
The Ritual of Autumn
Bergamot or rosemary oil, one golden or orange candle, clothes in bold colours, like gold, orange, red, green.
The Ritual of Winter
Oil of oranges, frankincense, cinnamon and ginger, dark clothes, one black or violet candle, paper and pen, a glass of water or a crystal sphere.

MOTHER MARY - *The Ritual of connecting with the Divine Mother*
First Ritual
Rose oil, aroma lamp, water bowl, one swimming candle, one candle (silver, pale blue or pale green), things which remind you of the power of the goddess like sea-shells, sand, starfish, pearls, flowers, ferns, leaves, crystals.

Second Ritual
One pink, green or pale blue candle, one white, pink and deep red rose, a small amount of sacred water, well water or sea water.

JESUS - *The Ritual of Connecting with the Divine Father*
A light and flowery essential oil, aroma lamp, one white candle, a chalice (or a beautiful drinking glass), water.

LADY PORTIA - *The Ritual of Initiation*
First Ritual
Patchouli, rosemary and lavender oil, black clothes, aroma lamp, amethyst, nine violet or black candles, one more candle, metal bowl with something underneath for heat protection.
Second Ritual
Patchouli, rosemary and lavender oil, black clothes, white clothes or robe, the same candles as in the first ritual, amethyst.

EL MORYA - *The Ritual of Protection*
Frankincense oil, fresh clothing, one white, silver, gold or violet candle, a little sage or lavender to burn.

KWAN YIN - *The Ritual of Compassion*
Neroli oil, white or pink clothes, one pale pink candle, items which induce compassion within you like photographs of animals or loved ones, aroma lamp or incense stick.

SAINT GERMAIN - *The Ritual of Transformation*
First ritual
One violet candle, one item which has to do with the situation to transform such as a wedding ring, a photograph.
Second ritual
Metal bowl with something underneath for heat protection, lavender oil, seven violet candles, paper and pen, lavender.

LADY NADA - *The Ritual of Joy*
Rosemary and rose-geranium oil, one pink candle, a chalice (or a beautiful drinking glass) wine or water, a little bread, one bunch of flowers or a single flower in a vase, a little bell.

DJWAL KHUL - *The Ritual of Serenity*
One white candle.

WOTTANA - *The Ritual of Connecting with the Earth*
A small personal item or a photo, a few grains of corn or a little tobacco.

ABOUT THE SYMBOLS

The following Ascended Master seals/symbols are two-dimensional representations of the Ascended Masters' energy, consciousness and vibration. They are keys: doorways and windows to the Lords and Ladies of Shambhala and can be used to call upon the Masters and the energetic manifestation of the Masters' special powers, presence and consciousness. They are completely safe for use as they are monitored over by the awareness of the Masters themselves. These symbols were channelled by Graham and Edwin Courtenay. Although these symbols are copyrighted, author and publisher permit use of them for private purposes, as long as there is no commercial interest. Please do credit the origins.

Brief Description of the Symbols

 LADY NIGHTINGALE
Two pentagonal figures in a circle. All light brown.

 SERAPIS BEY
The infinity symbol in a circle. All white.

 LADY MIRIAM
Equilateral triangle and one quadrangular (kite-shaped) figure in circle. All grass-green.

 KUTHUMI
Heart in a five-pointed figure in circle. All butter-yellow.

 MOTHER MARY
Two equilateral silver triangles (as the Star of David) in blue circle.

JESUS
Small circle and a T-form (stylising a human body)
in circle. All gold.

LADY PORTIA
Three equilateral violet triangles forming a star,
in a silver circle.

EL MORYA
Square on circle. All blue.

KWAN YIN
Flame in two squares in circle.
All opalescent pearl white.

SAINT GERMAIN
Seven pointed silver star in violet circle.

LADY NADA
Equilateral golden triangle and silver half moon
in golden circle.

DJWAL KHUL
Eight pointed star with a dot in the centre.
All turquoise.

WOTTANA
Four bent lines from top downwards and two
triangles, one pointing right, one pointing left in circle.
All light brown.

BY THE SAME AUTHOR:

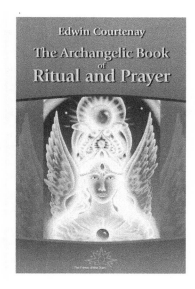

Edwin Courtenay
**The Archangelic Book
of Ritual and Prayer**

206 pages, paperback
ISBN 978-3-929345-27-8

Edwin Courtenay
**Reflections -
The Masters Remember**

167 pages, paperback
ISBN 978-3-929345-20-9